DANTE'S TRUNK

DANTE'S TRUNK

Ellen Hansa

Publisher: Ellen Hansa
website: transfiguration942.blog

First published in Australia 2022
This edition published 2022
Copyright © Ellen Hansa 2020, 2022

Cover design, typesetting: WorkingType (www.workingtype.com.au)

The right of Ellen Hansa to be identified as the Author of the Work has been asserted in accordance with the Copyright, Designs and Patents Act 1988.

All rights reserved. No part of this publication may be reproduced, stored in a retrieval system, or transmitted, in any form or by any means without the prior written permission of the publisher, nor be otherwise circulated in any form of binding or cover other than that in which it is published and without a similar condition being imposed on the subsequent purchaser.

Hansa, Ellen
Dante's Trunk
ISBN- 978-0-6455257-9-3

pp170

In loving memory of Ray.

THE TRUNK

Large, cumbersome, hard to move and incredible ugly in its coat of bright red with black stripes, Dante's Trunk ended up in Callan's care. It belonged to a magician with the name of Dante.

Originally the trunk was to be taken care of by Callan's friend, Tex, a country and western singer. Tex accepted an offer to travel with a Country and Western Show and left the large, heavy chest with Callan, promising to be back soon. Tex never came back, he disappeared into the Australian outback with his guitar. The responsibility of the trunk fell onto Callan. With great care he looked after it.

After his marriage to Lillie, he moved with his young family from Melbourne to the country. Dante's Trunk came along. Every time the family moved Callan and Lillie wondered what could be in it, what could make it so heavy? Callan decided to break the lock and opened the trunk. The whole family was curious what treasures there could be in the large, burdensome chest. The children dreamed of magical props, wondrous dress-ups, maybe there would be a wand? Surely the Magician Dante was not alive anymore? And where was Tex? Slowly they opened the lid. The children stood back in case some of the items were loaded with springs.

They were confronted with shoes, none of them matching. They were of the R.M. Williams variety; the ones with the elastic sides and a small heel, favoured by country folk. What magic does a man do with old, odd shoes? No one of the family could answer this question.

"Maybe Dante put a spell on the trunk. Maybe by opening the trunk the spell turned all the magic making things into shoes? Dad, you should not have opened the lid with such force! You woke up the Magic!" The three children looked angrily at their father.

There was also a biscuit tin containing beautiful old buttons. The shoes went to the tip, the children soon forgot their disappointment. They took the tin filled with the buttons and played with them for hours.

The now empty box became a home for Lillie and Callan's photographic enlargements. They had both been professional photographers. Every aspect of life was recorded. The enlargements, all of them black and white, were sorted and stored in boxes, which used to hold photographic paper. Each of them named and numbered, each full of memories.

BOX ONE

The words of her friends and family: "You will soon get over it", keep on echoing in her mind. How can she? He was supposed to be her partner for ever. For almost sixty years they had been together. Getting rid of all his clothes seem to make no difference. Selling his beloved piano does not help. The passing of time does not relieve the deep sorrow of her loss. Her grief has turned into anger, and fear. The fear comes at night, like a dark fog swerving around her, sitting on her, sucking her strength, creating deep panic by the thought of tomorrow, the thought of a future without him. The anger is with her all day. Anger for having been left alone. It was not meant to be like this!

She is filling her days with mindless work: like cleaning, polishing; polishing until everything is shining. Somehow the broom always takes her into his study. There she is confronted by Dante's Trunk, hiding under an old carpet. A wave of memories is welling up in her. The trunk also needs to go! Lillie tries to move it, but it sits there stubborn, glued to the floor. 'It must go', she thinks. She cannot understand why it is still here, why she has not removed it, and why she has not got rid of the life's memories it holds. Memories in the shape of photographs that fills the belly of this cumbersome monstrosity. She will deal with it tomorrow.

The next day Lillie goes ahead to empty Dante's Trunk. After lifting the lid, Callan's incredible sense of order confronts her. On the left, neatly stacked in long narrow boxes, the 4x4cm black-and-white negatives, kept in transparent numbered sleeves. Underneath the contact prints, sorted into subjects. The rest of the Trunk is filled with Agfa and Ilford boxes, which once held photographic paper. Each of them filled with photographs containing a part of her life with Callan, each of them a memory.

There was an Agfa box sitting on the top, making the order look untidy. It was marked 'Lillie', its bulging lid tied with string. She decides to undo the string, to look at the photos. The box is filled with memories of her childhood. She comes across an envelope with an Australian stamp.

"Things you keep!", she says to herself with a smile.

In the envelope is a birthday card from her big brother congratulating her on her tenth birthday. It is a splendid card of an elephant. He wiggles his bottom when it is opened and closed. After having played with the card for a while, Lillie reads the letter. It catapults her back to her childhood. She remembers how excited she was in reading the descriptions of the country her brother had moved to; the country where parrots fly free and strange animals carry their babies in a pocket. Those intoxicating snippets lured her, after her 21st birthday, to travel Down Under to the continent called, 'Australia'.

Lillie leans against Dante's Trunk and lets her mind wander back to the time when she was just twenty-one years old.

THE JOURNEY

Tired from her long trip and feeling lost, Lillie stood amongst the crowd of people in the large arrival lounge of the Melbourne Airport. She was frightened not to recognise her big brother. Ten years had passed since they saw each other. Watching groups of travellers being welcomed by friends and family increased her anxious feeling. The large arrival hall slowly emptied. Then a tall man in overalls walked towards her. His sleeveless, brown arms stretched out.

"Oh sis, I am so sorry to be late. I have come straight from work."

He lifted her up and gave her a hug, years fell away, old memories returned. Lillie feeling his strong arms around her, let go of all the fear she had felt throughout the flight. The memory of the interrogation by the immigration staff in Sydney dissolved. The way they were all put into cage-like enclosures, and the image of the poor migrants from the Eastern countries huddling together holding their meagre belongings, were forgotten. And the unbearable heat! Lillie buried her head into her brother's shoulder. She felt safe.

"Oh sis, it's so good to see you. Come let me help you. Is that all the luggage you have? Shall I help you with your little backpack?"

Lillie was clutching her small rucksack. She had been holding it tight all the way from Vienna. It contained all her papers, her photographic diploma, her passport, money, her two-year working visa, and a book her mother gave her to practice her English. Amongst the pages the card she got from her brother for her tenth birthday, the elephant card.

She felt strange in hearing English spoken all around her and embarrassed to speak it. But she had to try. She plucked up courage and started to speak:

"I have a big box coming. It has my photographic things in it. You know, pictures and my darkroom things. Also presents and little memories. It is a big wooden box. I was told in Sydney that it will come later to your house."

They were walking to the car park where Axel pointed at a large station wagon. He opened the back of the car and put Lillie's case on top of his tools. In Vienna Axel had trained as a cabinet maker. Here in his new country, he became a carpenter. Melbourne's building trade was booming. Slowly the town ate into the countryside. Suburb after suburb developed. Doncaster, where Axel lived with his family was such a suburb. The scars of the removed Apple Orchard still visible. A few trees huddled around an old weatherboard farmhouse. The new light-grey road went in a straight band through the naked landscape, past the old house and over the hill. At even distances driveways led to partially built houses, empty blocks of land, and some finished and occupied houses with newly created green lawns. The houses were boxed in on three sides by a solid-wooden fence.

Axel turned into one of the driveways. In the door of the pale-brick house stood a woman holding a baby, next to her a little boy. From the back of the house an old man appeared. With his work-hardened, nicotine-stained hands Grandad Anderson opened the car door for her.

"Welcome to Toronto Avenue. Welcome to Australia. Welcome, Love."

The woman slowly started to approach her. She put the baby on the grass and stretched out her hand.

"Welcome. Please do come in. I'll take your coat. You will not be needing it for a long time. I suppose it was cold in Vienna. Here it is the middle of summer. You have arrived in a heatwave!"

A welcoming smell of roast meat greeted Lillie as she entered.

"I hope you like lamb," Ruth said. "I thought I'd greet you with an Australian meal of roast lamb". Pointing towards the corridor she continued, "But I'm sure you would like to freshen up first. The bathroom is at the end of the passage. You're going to sleep in the room on the left."

Lillie could see Axel and young Nick struggling with the suitcase through the narrow doorway. Her room was tiny, there was just enough space for a single bed and a small table. The built-in wardrobes stretched along one side of the wall; her suitcase of clothes would never fill it. New curtains framed the window and the view, which was brought to a halt by a wooden fence. Above the new dark palings, the vastness of the Australian sky in the red evening light. She wondered what she would find behind the fence.

Lillie opened her case. On top, covering her clothes, a towel, under it the toiletry bag and a carefully folded summer dress, clean underwear and her slippers. Her mother had packed the case with love and thoughtfulness. Tears welled up as she thought of her parents two days away on the other side of the world.

"Look at you!", Axel made all eyes turn towards her as she entered the living room. "What a pretty sister I have!"

The family, apart from Ruth, who was in the kitchen, sat and watched the TV. Grandad got up and offered her a seat. In broken English, Lillie made them all aware that she could not understand what the person on the TV was talking about. She went into the kitchen and offered to help Ruth.

The following morning Lillie was pulled out of her sleep by the most beautiful birdsong. On the other side of the wooden fence, outside her window, a dead, old tree was stretching its black branches into the emerging daylight. On the very top of the tree sat a black-and-white bird warbling a song to the start of the day. Lillie felt it was a tune composed to welcome her first morning in her new country. It made her feel confident that all would be well.

Now she needed to find out what lay behind the wooden fence and beyond the new suburb of Doncaster, beyond the devastated landscape. She longed to see the wild Australia with its animals. But first she needed to get a job and with it her independence.

With a folder of folio prints and the certificate of her diploma in photography Lillie walked into Allan Studio in Smith St., Collingwood, Melbourne. The interview was short and easy and she got the job.

On her first working day she was introduced to the staff. Downstairs was ruled by Mavis, a large coarse woman. Lillie held her hand out for a greeting. Mavis ignored her outstretched hand and with a superior look on her face turned back to the work at her desk. The nickname of 'Desk-dragon' suited her well. Everything that came and went into Allan's Studio went via her. Nothing escaped Mavis.

The downstairs studios we're dedicated to advertising photography. Lillie was introduced to Hugo, Jim and Callan. All three of them welcomed her with warm handshakes. Hugo took her hand in both of his and asked, in a perfect Viennese dialect, how life in

Vienna was. He had come to Australia before the war, feeling the political unrest in Europe. He did not want to be called up to fight. Somehow, he did not escape the horrors of World War Two. Hugo, being classed as an enemy of the British Empire, was detained in a camp for the duration of the war. Jim and Callan had, just a few years ago, migrated from England.

"Ten Pound Poms," Callan said with a smile and a wink as he held her hand.

Lillie frowned. "Ten Pound Poms?"

Everyone laughed, Hugo explained.

"It means that they only paid £10 to get to Australia from England. They are also migrants; we are all migrants here! Except Mavis and the boss."

Having heard her name, Mavis stood up from behind her desk and with a booming voice told everyone to get back to work. She pointed at the stairs.

"You are going to work upstairs. Frank will show you around. I believe you like taking portraits. So, get upstairs and show us how good you are."

On the top of the stairs Frank was waiting for her. He shook her hand and whispered: "Don't worry about the old dragon too much. Her bark is worse than her bite."

Lillie smiled.

On creaking floorboards, they walked along a narrow corridor. The windows on the left looked out onto rusty tin-roofs. As they walked past doors Frank muttered:

"Children's studio. Here we take pictures of babies and children. Italian Dino is in charge of that." Frank pointed at the next door. "This will be your studio. And then further along the luncheon room, also used for washing and drying prints. Then at the end the darkroom. There is also a small room for developing all the negatives, but that is Hugo's domain."

He turned to the window and pointed at the view.

"And here the beautiful roofs of Collingwood. What a place! Welcome to Allan's Studio, the oldest studio in Melbourne. Can't you smell it?"

Frank took her into the lunchroom. A young woman stood by the drying machine waiting for prints to fall of the stainless-steel drum.

"Jenny, meet Lillie. She will be working in Portrait."

Jenny just smiled and continued putting the wet prints from the washing trough onto the belt of the dryer.

As Frank put the kettle on, he told Lillie that Jenny was the Studio's delivery-girl.

Over a cup of coffee Frank explained how everything worked on the first floor. Apparently, Mavis never came up, she hated climbing stairs. Lillie was told to keep out of Dino's way. He was a bad-tempered grump.

"Let's go and have a look at your domain." Frank held the door open for Lillie. She liked Frank. He was polite and he spoke slowly, so that she could understand what he said.

Walking into the middle of the portrait studio Frank waved his arms from equipment to equipment.

"We never change the lights. The boss thinks, no, he is convinced, that the settings of the lamps are perfect. We never remove the blind from the window. The natural light would upset the perfect lighting and we never touch the back drop it simply would fall apart."

Frank pointed at the large plate camera.

"The Monster!" He slightly bowed to the camera. "But I tell you it is the best piece of equipment in the whole studio. The cassettes will be loaded with film by Hugo. He also develops all the negatives.

The cassettes are in the cupboard over there."

Lillie looked at The Monster. She knew it well. The enormous camera mounted on wooden sturdy legs on wheels, with a crank handle to move the camera up and down. She remembered the nerve-wrecking way one had to expose the film by taking the lens cap off by hand, then counting the timing, then replacing the cap. Oh yes, she knew it well. They had the same camera at her photographic college in Vienna where Lillie had studied.

In the afternoon Lillie had to take a few passport photos. In case she needed some help, Frank was with her in the studio. In-between clients they talked about Europe. He had fled after the war from Yugoslavia into Austria and from there to Australia. His girlfriend's Sophie's family came from Poland.

"Melbourne is a city filled with people from all over the world. A very exciting place. You will see when you get to know this city."

Lillie soon learnt how to use the lights and the camera. Mavis was satisfied with her work. She fitted in with the group of workers upstairs and learnt to avoid contact with grumpy Dino.

One morning Frank brought a young Greek man into the studio. She had to take several portraits and one of the whole figure.

"The pictures will be sent to Greece to his wife-to-be. I think it is a terrible custom, brides chosen by photographs. We are after all in the twentieth century! One would think everyone would be allowed to marry for love. Please do your best."

She had to think of the Greek girls the plane had picked up in Athens during her flight to Sydney. Now Lillie understood why they all cried so much. They were leaving their homeland and family to start a life with a stranger in a foreign country. When arriving in Sydney the travellers were split up into groups and held in separate fenced in areas. She with a couple from Vienna, then the group of refugees from the eastern European countries and then all those young Greek women clutching a number. Brides by number! It made her shudder.

Lillie looked at the young man. He could not have been much older than herself. Like a soldier he placed himself on the podium in front of the camera, the old backdrop sadly hanging behind him with its nondescript pattern. Lillie tried to get him to relax. Slightly frustrated and extremely embarrassed Lillie demonstrated the pose she was trying to get him to achieve. In her school English she asked him to put one hand in his trouser pocket and then slightly turn his upper body towards the camera and then to look into the lens.

"Anything else?" he asked in a frustrated voice.

Lillie felt the blood rise. Then they both laughed.

"No, I am just trying to make you look relaxed and natural, like that."

She stood next to him on the podium again showing him what kind of pose she wanted him to achieve. He copied her. She liked the way he looked; he looked very handsome. She smiled at him and took the picture.

The next day she was called to the desk. There was Mavis plus a woman dressed in black and the young man waiting for her. The proofs of her work were laid out in front of her.

"Why did you put his hand in his pocket?" Mavis barked. "The girl will think there is something wrong with his hand!"

The Greek lady nodded; the young man smiled at Lillie. It was an embarrassed smile. It was a good picture; there was nothing wrong with it.

"I will get Hugo to retake it and maybe he can teach you how it is done," Mavis said dismissively.

'Maybe I should have photographed him in his birthday suit,' Lillie thought as she walked away. 'Then the bride could see that he is faultless!'

Full of disappointment Lillie walked past the portrait studio towards the darkroom. Dino had taken over her job. She was going to continue her employment at Allan Studio in the dark room. Lillie was also slightly angry. For the weeks she had worked as a portrait photographer she had no complaints. Mavis even sometimes congratulated her.

With dread she entered the small room that dealt as a light-lock and from there into the stuffy darkroom. It took a while for her to adjust to the darkness. One wall seemed to have a long bench with red lights over it. 'Developer trough', Lillie thought. Out of the dark Callan called her. Carefully, so that she would not trip over the old floorboards, she walked towards the sound. Her eyes started to adjust to the red glow. Callan showed her the enlarger she was going to use.

Running her fingers over the enormous enlarger, Lillie realised that it was the same as they had at the college in Vienna. She wondered where Allan's Studio managed to get all this old equipment from.

The negative was already in the enlarger. Lillie tried to find the timer-clock. Callan laughed when she asked him where it was.

"Sorry love, no timer. Can you hear the loud ticking? Each tick one second. For this lot you will need ten seconds. You will have to count."

He turned the enlarger on and there was a lady with long flowing hair waiting to be turned into a positive print. They had a large job for 'Her Majesty's Theatre' to be completed by tomorrow. All the enlargers in the darkroom were pumping out smiling faces of actors.

Callan showed her where to find the photographic paper and

disappeared into the reddish light. Out of the dark she could hear him call:

"Fifty prints of that lady. Can you do a ten-pack? Developing ten prints in one go? Just call out if you need a hand."

Yes, Lillie could do a ten-pack. She turned off the enlarger light and placed a sheet of paper into the printing frame. She made one print and took it over to her developer, where she looked for rubber gloves or tongs to develop the print.

"Any gloves or tongs?"

"No Love, just use your hands."

Shuddering at the thought of having to put her hands in the chemical mix of the developer Lillie got on with her job.

By lunchtime she had finished her fifty prints and was given a new negative.

Although she knew the enlarger well, Lillie felt nervous in changing negative in the dark. She did not want to ask for help; she would have to learn how to do it. On her first day in the darkroom, she did not want to make mistakes, but she did.

"Sorry, I have just dropped a negative."

Reassuring Callan's voice came out of the red gloom:

"Don't worry love! Just stay where you are, so that you do not walk on the negative." And he asked the others in the room to pack up their paper.

"Great excuse for a smoko!"

The lights came on and showed a large, black-painted room. Everything was painted black. There were four enlargers, all the same make and age. On the far wall a large clock-like contraption ticking away. Along one wall a wooden trough lined with tin sheeting in which the developer dishes stood on heating boxes. The wooden edge of the trough and the floor were overgrown with thick fluffy chemical crystals. Only where workers rubbed up against the bench could one see the rotting timber framing. There were no exhaust fans to remove the fumes of the chemicals.

"Mein Gott!" Lillie called out. "This will all make us very sick!"

She picked up her negative and, with horror in her thoughts, continued her job. This was not a place where she wanted to continue on working.

There was a job going at the Melbourne University Zoology Department. Lillie felt she had the right qualifications and applied for the position. Knowledge in macro and micro photography was paramount. The two years she had worked in Oslo at an Institute for Industrial Research as a photographic-assistant and the portfolio she had brought with her, should get her the job.

Professor Burnstock was leading Lillie along a seemingly endless corridor, which took her past a number of rooms. At the very end she was greeted by a large well-lit space with work benches under sizeable windows which were looking out into trees. First, he showed Lillie her workspace. The darkroom was small and compact one third was occupied by a low table on which an enlarger-looking contraption was mounted. On closer inspection Lily realised that it was a macro camera for taking close-ups. Then on a higher bench, a new looking enlarger with an automatic timer, underneath drawer for photographic paper. The developing area was covered in stainless steel. There was no window in the small room. When turning on the red lights an exhaust fan which, was situated over the developer, came on automatically. Lillie was thrilled she would be the boss of her own small dark room. Jeff Burnstock smiled as he watched Lillie run her hand along the benches.

"There is a white lab coat hanging at the back of the door. I hope we got the right size for you. Melita will tell you all about the ins and outs of this part of the department. Come down to my office before you go. We can then discuss what I will be expecting from you."

Jeff closed the door behind him leaving Lillie in the dimly lit space. She put on the white lab coat. Throwing her arms in the air Lillie did a little dance of joy.

"My own dark room," she quietly sang to herself. "My very own space."

A gentle knock on the door brought her back to the fact that she was not alone in the department. Opening the door, she had to adjust to the bright light of the window opposite. Lillie was overwhelmed by a big hug.

"Oh. Mein liebes Kind, wie ist Wien?"

Melita stepped back and held Lillie at arm's length. A pair of wet eyes looked at Lillie. The woman was in her late fifties, about as tall as Lillie, with a mop of curly, unmanageable white hair which framed her head against the light of the window like a halo. Overwhelmed Lillie stepped back into her domain and muttered: "Danke, Wien ist schön."

Behind Melita stood a young, very tall man. He slowly and gently pushed Melita out of the doorway and invited Lillie to step out of the darkroom.

"John, John McKlean and this is Melita Pertinac. Melita is our pathologist, I am her assistant. I also am studying genetics here at the Uni. Please come and sit down with us and tell us all about Vienna. Melita has been terribly homesick all these years she has been in Australia. She came out during the war which took everything away from her. She told me her family's house outside of Vienna was destroyed by a bomb. But I am sure she will tell you all about it."

He pulled out a chair for her.

"Would you like a cup of tea? I'll get one from the canteen."

Melita just stood and looked at Lillie, who started to feel embarrassed.

"I am sorry staring at you, mein liebes Kind, but I do not meet many people from Vienna. Give me one more hug and I will leave you alone!"

Lillie and Melita remained the best of friends until Melita's death in 2015. Any difficult situation, and Melita was there to help and to advise.

Jeff Burnstock sat behind his big desk when Lillie went to see him. He was a good-looking man in his late or maybe mid-fifties. Everything about him was trim; his small beard and tightly curled, black hair; his clothes of excellent quality. On the desk Lillie noticed photographs of his family. One could see that they were taken in a studio. 'Maybe Allan's Studio?' Lillie thought. There was also a beautifully carved wooden sculpture. Lillie remarked on the photos.

"Well, maybe one day you can photograph my family? These are rather outdated. I see you like the sculpture. It is one of mine. I like carving wood. It is a very satisfying and relaxing hobby."

He smiled moving the sculpture closer to Lillie.

"But to you and the work we will be expecting from you."

The main bulk of her work would be to make slides for talks by the department's lecturers. Prints had to be made for reproductions in magazines. The microscopic photographs were being taken by the researchers. The rolls of film would be delivered to her to be processed. Lillie nodded to show that she had understood.

"Every job has a deadline! And I must warn you sometimes the researchers here want the work done by yesterday. You might find yourself at some stage having to do overtime. Melita will show you how we like the prints done."

He gave her another of his charming smiles.

"And now it is time to go home. See you tomorrow."

Lillie kept up contact with her friends from Allan's Studio. With them she discovered Melbourne's nightlife. She was introduced to clubs in St. Kilda. Acland Street was almost like a home coming for Lillie. The Viennese cake shop and Café Scheherazade. Especially Café Scheherazade where she could indulge in a bowl of Goulash soup and Rye Bread. But Lillie was longing to see the Australia she had dreamed of. She wanted to see a Kangaroo and the large white parrots her brother had told her about. She wanted to see the Eucalyptus forests. The exotic places her friends called the Bush and the Outback.

After one of Sophie's many parties Lillie sat in the dark in the tiny backyard of her friend looking at the small square of sky between the buildings.

"Look at this sky. So many stars." She mumbled to herself. "I have seen nothing of this country, except Doncaster and a bit of Collingwood and Carlton and St. Kilda."

"I'll show you."

Callan stood beside her.

"Yes, I'd like to show you. We can do daytrips over the Easter holidays. We could go a few miles up north, maybe into the Victorian Alps or down to the sea?".

BOX TWO

Should she open it and let the past out?

Holding on to the yellow Ilford box, she smiles. His favourite photographic paper.

For a long time, she looks at the box. The beginning of her new life, so long ago, yet still imprinted in her psyche. The love of a new land. The love of a man she had just lost.

She looks at the black-and-white print. It is a picture of bleached ghost-gums against a dark hill. At the edge of the trees a small farmhouse, looking alone and empty. She smiles as she remembers.

A NEW LAND

Feeling slightly uneasy by the thought of the day ahead, Lillie lay in bed and watched the dawn. The dead tree outside her window had been cut down. The block next door had been sold. Her beloved magpie lost the stage from where she could perform her morning song. The bird's warble had been replaced by the noise of machinery.

But it was Sunday, and everything was quiet. Lillie was thinking of her outing with Callan. She did not really know him. What if she did not like him! What if he tried to be too friendly? On the other hand, she thought, it was only for the day, and she wanted so much to see the Australian countryside. Maybe they would spot a kangaroo. This thought wiped out her anxiety.

In the kitchen Ruth was preparing breakfast.

"I am making some sandwiches for you to take. Also, would you like a thermos of tea? You will need to take a bottle of water. It is going to be hot again. You must also take a jacket, just in case. Our weather is very changeable."

She turned towards Lillie:

"What is Callan all about?"

Lillie had to admit that she only knew him from Allan's Studio.

"He is from England, a migrant. But he keeps on talking about going back to England. He has done his two years in Australia and is looking forward in getting back to, what he calls, the Old Country. He is nice and helped me a lot to fit into work."

Embarrassed Lillie made herself busy checking her camera bag. Ruth smiled as she put the food into Lillie's small backpack.

"Well, it is only for one day and then you did want to get out into the bush? I am sure you will have an enjoyable day."

From the front garden Axel was calling Lillie.

"There is a strange looking, big, old car coming up the road. It must be your transport! Goodness me what kind of a car is it?"

A very large grey car, stripped of all its chrome trimmings turned into the driveway. Lillie ran back into the house to get her things; the rest of the household stood and stared, wondering what the driver was all about. Little Nick ran to Callan as he stepped out of the car.

"Look what Easter bunny brought me. Lots and lots of chocolate eggs! Look! Would you like one?"

Callan ruffled the boy's hair, smiled, and took one of the brightly wrapped chocolate eggs.

"Thank you, I'll have that with my morning tea."

Axel looked over the car and wondered if it was safe and what sort of car it was. Also, he wanted to know where Callan was going to take his little sister.

"I thought we might drive to Mount Baw Baw, show Lillie that we have some mountains here in Victoria. This old lady is a 1948 Dodge. No worries, she will get us there and back. I am in the throes of renovating her."

As Lillie climbed into the enormous front seat of the car, Axel had a stern word with Callan to make sure that he brought his sister home in one piece.

She had never been far out of Melbourne. The countryside, the open spaces, the trees! What impressed her the most were the mountain ash; so tall and straight. It felt like driving through a cluster of tall pillars holding up a green roof. The forest floor was covered in ferns, small shrubs and young trees. Often, they stopped to take photographs. They drove alongside a valley with a little farmhouse. It looked dwarfed with the mountain rising behind it. On the slopes, like skeletons, stood the remnants of large trees: white, sharp and very photogenic.

"Ghost gums; weather-bleached, dead eucalypts."

They stopped and took a photo. The sun did not reach the mountainside. Only the trees and the little house were touched by the rays of the sun, creating a strange eerie feeling in the landscape. Before Lillie could ask why the trees had died, Callan had started the car and was ready to drive on, into yet another magnificent part of the landscape.

On top of Mount Baw Baw, they found a great spot for a picnic. Table and benches were provided, but they both decided to walk further, where they found some great boulders to sit on. The view over the landscape below them took Lillie's breath away. All around her flowers. They were small, hugging the ground, hiding from the mountain wind, they reminded Lillie of the flowers she had seen in the Austrian Alps, small and hardy.

"Tomorrow we will go down to the sea."

He pointed.

"It is somewhere in that direction"

They slowly ate their lunch and talked about their dreams and wishes.

"When I've done up the Dodge, I'll sell her and get myself a ticket back home to England. I have had enough of Australia. I hate Melbourne! It is so ugly! I miss the ancient buildings and the history of my country. And the terrible customs here! Closing pubs at 6 pm. And the way the people drink, as if there was no tomorrow. Give me an English pub any day, and English beer!"

Lillie was shocked, waving her arms, making a gesture as if she was drawing a curtain. She looked out over the hills bathed in a grey-blue haze. They were soft and round. Not like the mountains in her country, sharp and jagged.

"But what about the magic of this landscape?"

"Landscape is not all, love!"

'Love?' she thought. 'Why do people call me, 'love'? I am not his love.'

His attitude saddened Lillie. To her this new country was full of excitement, the chance to a new future, to everything new! Would she become disillusioned after having been in this country for a few years?

Their drive back was a quiet one. Each in their own thoughts. Callan was dreaming of England, of a country steeped in history and what he thought of as civilised customs. Lillie dreamed of the Australian bush with its wild feelings and open spaces. Most of all she dreamed of the freedom this country will give her.

Back in Toronto Avenue he thanked her for a great day, held her hand and winked.

"See you tomorrow, love?"

"Yes, great. I'll bring lunch."

"Don't worry. We'll pick up something on the way."

As Callan drove off, Axel came out of the house.

"How was your day, sis?"

"Why do people call you 'Love', when they don't love you?"

"Because they don't remember your name," Ruth laughed.

For some reason Wilsons Promontory was closed and they ended up at Cape Liptrap. The tide was out, perfect for beachcombing. Lillie had taken off her shoes to feel the fine sand. Her feet had not ever felt sand like that. This was the first beach she had walked on. Squeezing the sand between her toes, Lillie ambled to the edge of the water. Callan had been right the water was freezing! He had told her that there was only a place called Tasmania between them and the South Pole. She strained her eyes to find the island of Tasmania on the horizon. All Lillie could see was water and more water. 'It must be the ocean,' she thought as she stepped out of the water onto the warm sand. With her eyes peeled onto the ground, Lillie carried on along the beach looking for treasures the waves had deposited on the sand. Just before arriving at the end of the small bay, she found the skull of an albatross. It was only the top part of the head, including the distinguished strong beak with the curved tip. What a treasure! Carefully she put it with the shells and small pieces of driftwood into her sunhat.

Heading back, she saw nothing of her companion. He had wandered off in the opposite direction. The end of the beach did not stop him. Callan had climbed over the rocks to see if he could find something there.

Lillie sat in the sand sorting out the shells from the driftwood, putting the skull of the bird safely in the middle of a ring of small stones. She was in her very own world creating pictures with her found treasures. What should she take, what leave behind?

'He is probably going to laugh at me. They all did back home,' she thought. No one of her friends could see the beauty in the small object's nature had put in front of them. Lillie picked up one of the round pebbles, feeling its smoothness.

"What a lovely collection you have got there!" Callan startled her. He was holding up a broken shell she had found.

"Look at this. Is it not beautiful? Nature is just so clever. Look at the inside, like a spiral staircase. And look at that one. Just imagine that enlarged. It would make a great sculpture. Did I tell you I studied sculpture at Art School in England? Show me, show me what else you got, what a beautiful lot. Look at that skull!"

He held the head by the beak, stretched out his arm and looked at it. Then turned it sideways, then with the beak up.

"Beautiful! Nature is just so clever."

There was a different person in front of her, a different Callan. He was so excited about nature's gems. Back in Vienna her friends had called her found treasures rubbish and stuff. She looked out at the endless sea, watching the waves lap the sand. Her thoughts on the other side of the world, remembering.

"A penny for your thoughts?"

He shook her out of her reflections.

She watched him play with her stones and shells, turning them into patterns. Then suddenly he got up. Looking around he found a flat stone and placed the skull on it.

"There, the best of the bunch," he said, winking at her.

Lillie just stared at him.

She had hardly noticed him when first introduced. Just the way he had dressed in the dull, well-worn old clothes, his strange mannerism. Suddenly he looked different. He had taken his sunglasses off and looked at her. She saw his sort of grey-blue eyes, cheeky, yet at the same time quiet and serious. His mousy-brown, slightly curly, untidy hair; the white shirt with the sleeves turned up just below the elbows.

They looked at each other. Both felt a deep connection between them.

Lillie got embarrassed and started fiddling with her newly found gems the sea had deposited on the beach for her. She was trying to decide what to take.

"I will definitely take the bird-skull."

"Why not take the lot?"

"No, they belong here."

They sat together watching the tide come in and the waves splash against the rocks. She felt that she knew him from somewhere, a feeling of deja vu.

"Time to go," broke the stillness, the comfortable feeling in her.

"Yes, better get going".

Meeting for lunch at *'Pellegrini', a small cafe-restaurant not far from the Melbourne University, had become a daily event.*

Lillie and Callan's friendship grew from day to day. He was still thinking about going back to England. They sat and ate their small bowl of pasta, drank a good cup of coffee, talked and talked. The conversation flowed in and out of all kinds of subjects. Often Callan would talk about his days as a boy in Stoke-on-Trent, the beauty of the landscape in the Midlands and the excitement of the history of his home country.

"Back home, you know, I just used to jump the fence into the neighbour's field," Callan said. "Beyond was a forest with an overgrown, forgotten factory. It was falling apart, and we children had an exciting, adventurous time there. In the deeper, constantly filled water holes lived all kinds of small creatures. I loved watching the newts. Sometimes, when I was lucky, I managed to catch a grass snake, put it down my sleeve and bring it home. In the old machinery birds would find nesting places. These ruins were from the beginnings of the Industrial Revolution, a fascinating time in British history. You see I miss the feeling of history. In this country I cannot see it, cannot feel it!".

Lillie could not understand. This new country was so full of exciting things. Everything was new. Everything was different. Callan had already been in Australia for two years. He could not see the beauty anymore. His Midland-English accent made him amongst the Australians a laughingstock. They called him a Pommy Bastard! All he wanted was to go back to civilised England with its history.

She never wanted to go back to war-torn Europe, to Vienna with its bombed-out houses. She could do without that kind of past.

As they kept on meeting for lunch, Callan started to mellow. Their friendship grew and his homesickness lessened.

———◆———

When Tom the cat came into Lillie's life, she had to move out of Toronto Avenue. Ruth despised cats. Vermin, she called them. Lillie saw the little black kitten in the University car park and when it was still there in the evening, she brought it home. Tom learnt to live in her car. The car became his home. Lillie had to find them a new place to live.

The room in an old weatherboard house belonging to a pensioner, became their new home. Even in summer the damp room was cold. There was safe parking, off-road, for her precious newly bought car, an old Ford Prefect and Tom was allowed in the house. The view from her window was through an unkempt garden onto a busy road. There were no birds waking her up, only the constant hum of the traffic. In her small room the tiny iron grate in the fireplace was broken and had been replaced by a two-bar electric heater. The heater doubled as a toaster. Lillie disliked using the kitchen. The old man always sat at the table in his dressing gown, amongst the dirty plates, slurping his cup of tea, listening to the races. With the electric heater turned on its side and an electric kettle Lillie was set up to cook a simple meal in her room. Almost every day after work Callan would come to Essendon for a visit.

One day he arrived with a large paper-bag full of cheeses, biscuits and a bottle of fine wine. Having spread one of Lillie's towels on the floor, he created a banquet. Tom being extremely interested in the spread of food was put outside. Lillie fetched two glasses from the kitchen.

Callan lifted his glass. "Prosit! Cheers! A drink to US."

They clinked their glasses.

"What's the occasion?" she asked.

Long did Callan look at her.

"Would you marry me?"

Lillie blushed and stepped away from him.

"Marry? No, I never want to get married! I need to be free, to follow my dream, I need to be independent, get on with my photographic career; maybe even fulfil my great wish of becoming a photo-journalist. I do not want to be anyone's wife, having a bundle of children, making lunch and dinner, staying at home. No, I could not do that!".

Giving him a hug, she did say that she liked him very much, as a friend, as a special friend. Marriage was a big commitment a solid bind. Lillie was not sure, if she was ready for marriage.

With a slightly disappointed smile Callan looked hard at Lillie.

"What about if I secure your friendship by buying you? Would one shilling be enough? If you give me pen and paper, I can write up a contract. Tom could witness the purchase. This would only be a very loose bind."

The document is still amongst Lillie's important papers. Stored away next to her birth certificate and the papers of her photographic diploma. It lies with his death certificate and her will.

They had become lovers. There was no talk about going back to England or a career as a photographer. On weekends they packed up the Dodge with tent, food and Tom and took off up-country, searching out new places.

BOX THREE

Tears stream down her face. The tattered photo of her and Callan with the old Dodge stare at her. For many years it was pinned above her writing desk. Lillie regrets having treated it so badly; having pulled it off the wall; not wanting to remember the beautiful days they spent on that trip. Carefully she flattens the photo. Through a curtain of tears, it floated in front of her. But then she does not need her eyes, she can almost smell the memories the pictures evokes in her. The smell of the Outback. Never will she forget the dry landscape, the vastness of her new country. The first night she spent under the splendid stars of the Australian night sky.

She dabbles at the tears with a tissue. She nods. Yes, she will go back to this memory; look at these pictures.

UP COUNTRY

Through a friend they managed to rent a flat in an old mansion in Carmyle Avenue, Toorak. The upstairs part of Carmyle House had been savagely cut up into flats. Two of the larger rooms seemed to be still in their original state, with large fireplaces and doors leading onto a veranda with a view into parts of the old gardens of the once grand house. The distinguished feeling of the place disappeared when getting to the kitchen and bathroom. The kitchen was long and narrow. When standing in the middle of the room one could almost touch both sides of the wall. On one side it was equipped with an extremely old gas stove, on the other a sink and bench. Under the window a small table. From there one looked directly into next-door's enormous Magnolia tree, a view that made Lillie forget the unpleasant environment of the kitchen. By placing their two beautifully decorated, old plates and mugs, and a few pots on the shelves Lillie made the kitchen theirs.

Callan had found the plates in a second-hand shop and immediately recognised their country of origin. Pointing at the mark on the back he smiled.

"They were made in the same place as me, Stoke-on-Trent, the heart of the potteries."

Amongst a pile of second-hand furniture Lillie had found an old chair. "Handmade by a Dutch migrant," the shop owner told her.

"I'll have it. A chair would be very useful and this one is certainly quite special." She looked at Callan and said with a cheeky laugh: "Made in Holland! That is just a bit down the road from where I was made, in Austria."

Callan discovered an old, ornate wind-up clock. He declared that the ticking would keep them good company, also it will tell them the time. With a few planks and bricks, he built a bookshelf to accommodate his collection of novels. Wooden boxes and an old broomstick created a place for their clothes. Dante's Trunk, covered in a cloth, served as a table. A few cushions by the fireplace gave them a cosy living space. The summer evenings they would sit on the spacious veranda looking over the old gardens of the posh neighbourhood. And so, they had made the rooms in the old mansion their own.

The clip-clop of the milkman's horses woke Lillie up. Carmyle Avenue was a cul-de-sac and the horse and cart had to be slowly manoeuvred. Lillie had the same problem when steering her old Ford Prefect around the small turnaround. The posh neighbourhood had complained about the state of both hers and Callan's car. Her beloved Ford had a big-end-problem and when accelerating sounded like a sewing machine on steroids. Callan had already fixed the exhaust. He told her that the old girl was on her way out, she was dying. But Lillie needed her car to get to work. Sometimes, when there was a special order to go out, she had to be at work early.

The smell of baked cheese sandwiches greeted Lillie as she opened the door into the flat. Callan was surprising her with his special meal. Having just got home from work, Lillie kicked off her shoes. She was dead tired. Callan handed her a glass of wine and invited her to sit down by the fire.

"I'll never be able to get up if I settle down in the cushions. We are flat out at work. I am buggered! Also, tomorrow I will have to work overtime. Prof. Burnstock is giving a talk somewhere. He needs slides, slides and more slides."

Giving her a big comforting hug Callan lead her to a map of Australia which he prominently had displayed on the floor. Next to it a letter.

"I got a letter from my mate Bill. He is working at a sheep station called 'Koonamore'. I am trying to find it on the map. It is somewhere near Broken Hill."

He smiled and asked if she was too tired to listen to his story about Bill. Lillie had settled down by the fire. With a nod, she encouraged him to go ahead.

"Together we travelled all over NSW in his old Chevy, towing my big caravan. We had a great time. He played the guitar and I the fiddle. 'Click Goes the Shears', '10-000 Miles Away', 'Danny Boy', and lots more. We played for beer. My God our singing and playing was bad. But fun? Did we have fun!

One day we drove past a homestead with an old Chevy parked in the front yard. The bonnet was up, and a very large backside bulged out of it. Bill stopped to help. I could smell a roast. The old man was sitting on the veranda, drinking, surrounded by bottles. The backside under the bonnet belonged to his wife. One of the kids came out of the house, asking mum for advice about the roast. She stuck her head up and let go the foulest language."

'Need any help?' Bill asked.

She stopped shouting and looked at him.

"Youse a Chevy man?'

Straightening up she put her hands on her hips. She was a hard-looking woman, a real outback hag.

'And what do you want in return?'

'The roast smells rather grand!'

'Oh, bugger off!' she snarled.'"

Callan laughed and pointed at the food on the trunk. He was an expert in toasted cheese sandwiches.

"Sorry, love, no roast. I also made a sort of a salad."

Handing Lillie her plate he continued: "You should get some time off for all the overtime you have given your good Professor. Why don't you ask him? We could go up and see my mate and you might even see a kangaroo. Also, my love, you will experience the real Australian outback."

The endless straight road to Yunta, cutting through the immeasurable vast landscape made Lillie feel very small. The country appeared to be going on forever; so large, so endless and so flat. It seemed to her that the land and sky were divided by an absolutely straight line. Sharp and straight, with the road in the middle looking like a perfect geometric drawing. She felt as if the land would swallow them up at the narrow part where highway met horizon. She understood how the ancient people thought the Earth was flat. The sky was so blue and vast, the earth purple-brown and later terracotta red. Small blue-grey shrubs were dotted throughout this barren, yet beautifully powerful landscape.

They stopped to photograph this view, but no photograph could do justice to the vastness of this empty landscape. She would have to carry the image in her head and heart.

Lillie was looking for a clump of shrubs or a small grove of trees.

"Nowhere to go for a wee?" Lillie asked.

"Yes, you go on this side of the car and I on the other," he replied.

Tom the cat followed Lillie. He seemed to understand. He dug his little hole and got the catty meditative look, as cats do when they have a pee. As soon as Tom had covered his hole he was back in the safety of the car, like a black streak, and settled in the rear window.

The car purred, feeling the freedom of speed, having the cobwebs from the city blown away. Callan pulled the throttle out. He put his feet on the dashboard. She flew along at 80 miles per hour on the never-ending straight road. They met no one. Not a car, not a sheep: nothing. The road kept its perfect geometric shape. The car never seemed to get to the narrow part of it. Sometimes there was a gentle dip in the road, like a soft wave.

"Bill once did the country postal run. He never met a car in days. When stopping for a rest he stuck his hat on a stick and started conversing with it. He felt that in those days his hat was his best friend, and so useful!"

Lillie looked at the never-ending emptiness. 'Postal run? Where to? To whom?' She strained her eyes trying to see the roof of a house or a gate leading to a driveway. Eventually she gave up, relaxed into the comfortable seat and fell asleep. Suddenly the car veered to the right, then straight and then left. It woke her up.

Callan laughed: "They call it a 'dog-leg'. It stops you from falling asleep."

The car settled back to its comfortable speed. Callan relaxed and put his feet back on the dashboard. The sun was getting low. The landscape changed colour.

"I don't think we will make it to Yunta," he said. "We'd better look out for a spot to camp."

Just before sunset the tent was up and the campfire lit. Lillie was mesmerised by the play of colour. The ground had turned a brilliant red. It seemed that the sun and the campfire were having a challenge over their strength in the intensity of the vibrant colours. Later the fire and the sun were almost one and the same. Sitting on the ground gave her a new perspective. The sky was now so vast, the horizon slightly curved, the grey-blue saltbush very prominent with just a bit of the red soil showing. Here and there the skeleton of a dead tree would cut its black lines into the sky.

"Which tin shall we open tonight?" Callan shook Lillie out of her thoughts. "We can have spaghetti with pasta sauce?"

"Yes, whatever," was her response.

Callan had put the pots on the fire.

"I cook, you do the dishes, that's the rule of the house."

They watched the sun disappear behind the saltbush. Just a few orange-red sparks through the foliage and then she was gone, leaving an orange-purple glow. Behind them the night sky, slowly moving, covering the light of the day. But the sun was not going to be put out that quickly. The afterglow turned the horizon into a colour spectacle Lillie had never seen before.

"Just like Edvard Munch saw the sky that inspired him to paint, 'The Scream'. The scream of the day as night puts it out," Lillie murmured. "How beautiful!"

Then came the night. There was no moon, just blackness with millions of little white dots.

"Look", Callan said, "There is the Southern Cross."

They lay on their backs looking up into the vastness of the sky. Callan showed Lillie the constellations. But Lillie did not listen. She just felt the ancient earth underneath her, smelled the dry, now cool, air and then this endless sky above. Her spirit had gone to a new place, a place she had not been before. And she felt she could not be any happier.

"If I died now," she said. "I die as happy as one can be!"

"Don't you do that! There's another exciting day in front of us."

Next morning there were still a few embers in the fire. Lillie and Tom went on their morning call. The sun was still behind the horizon, there was just the first glow visible. She thought of a children's story her mother had read to her. Somewhere in the story the sun was getting ready for her daily entrance, her arrival. The story told how the sun took a long time to appear. She needed to be quite sure to be as beautiful as she could be, as impressive as possible. There was no competition from clouds this morning. Lillie watched her rise; slowly, majestic, calculating. The sun brought colour back into the landscape; red, blue and grey.

On the way back to camp Lillie collected some wood and got the fire going again. The billy-can had been sitting next to the embers and was near boiling. A cup of tea for Callan and then she was off with her good friend, the camera, trying to record the feeling of the landscape.

The smell of cooked breakfast lured her back to the camp. Tom was licking the last crumbs from his bowl. Callan was cooking toasted cheese sandwiches, one of their favourites.

Yunta was just, 'up the road'. They did not linger. Koonamore was calling. After having turned off the highway onto a dirt road the landscape changed a bit. The road was rough and the driving slow. It became slightly hilly, just sort of bumps in the landscape. Along a straight stretch of road, they saw buildings. No, it was not the sheep station. It was an empty town. The missing buildings made the village look like a toothless mouth. They parked the car outside a house. A sign on the gate said: 'Trespassers will be prosecuted.' Then a name and the date of 1940-something. Lillie shuddered. 1940! She was not even born then! On one corner stood a very large building.

It was surrounded by a high fence. 'Waukaringa Pub' was written on one side.

"This is a very creepy place," Lillie said to Callan, who had found a dried-up dead dog or dingo. He was taking photos of it. After clearing an area of stones Callan lay down on the ground, taking a picture of the gaping mouth of the dried-up animal. In the background the ruins of the pub.

"This is a fascinating place," Callan replied. "And so photogenic!"

"What is this place? It is rather eerie."

"It is a ghost town."

"Have you been to a place like this before?"

"Well, there are many deserted houses in the outback. People looking for grazing land, built homesteads or a town and then the rain stopped, and the land died, and with it their livestock. They moved on or perished. There are also a number of ghost towns from the goldrush days. When the gold runs out, they need to leave. This could be the case here. Look, there's a very large chimney in the distance. Let's go around the back of this house and see what we can find."

Cameras in hand they started to explore.

Lillie walked behind one of the houses. There was an old, rusty T-model Ford parked at the back. The shade-cloth on the veranda hung tattered and seemed to be the only thing moving in the breeze. The sun started to get some strength. The heat seemed to be making the place even more deserted.

It appeared that someone had been sleeping on the back veranda. There was an old mattress and unmade dirty bedding. It made Lillie shudder, still she ventured on. The only noise was the one she made on the old floorboards and the flapping of the shredded shade-cloth. The flywire door, with its ornate finishes, was without the wire, but not locked. The door also was unlocked. Lillie found herself in the kitchen. The room was completely untouched. It felt as if the owners had just gone down to the shops for some milk. It was spotless. Just the dust from all those years of it being unoccupied, unloved, covered everything in an even blanket. A tea towel hung on the back of the chair.

Callan joined Lillie. She grabbed his hand.

"I am out of here. This is spooky!"

She quietly turned around, so quiet as not to wake the inhabitants. Outside she found something to sit on, somewhere in the sun. She felt cold. 'What happened here? Where have all the people gone?' she thought.

Suddenly, she felt someone watching her. On the same side of the pub was a stone house and in the shade of the veranda stood an old man looking at her. And then he was gone. The place returned to its emptiness; now feeling even more so. The sun did not warm her up. She went to the car to fetch a jumper. Tom was hiding under the seat.

'Animals know when something is not as it should be,' she thought.

Callan was off taking pictures of the pub.

"It must have been quite a big place. This was a big pub."

One wall had fallen over, and they could see the bedrooms, all painted in a different colour.

"I wonder if this was an outback brothel, each lady with an exotic name in her exotic room. This is crazy. Pity we can't go in."

Callan rattled on the gate, but it did not give way.

Further down the street, so empty of people and houses, was a store. Its veranda had fallen off. For safety the windows had been covered in boards. They peered through the broken glass panels of the door. On both sides of the room were shelves stacked with one thing and another. A large, partially broken counter ran alongside one wall. At the end a large door, wide open, framing the desolated, flat landscape.

"Probably a grocer", Callan said.

The sun had crept high in the sky. The shadows became short, the landscape flat. Waukaringa felt more deserted. It was time to move on.

The old Dodge took the bad dirt road like a ship on a choppy sea; she seemed to float over the corrugations. The bigger dips felt like larger waves. In the distance they could see a gate. As they came closer there was a sign, crudely handwritten without artistry. It said: 'Koonamore'. Callan stopped the car and took out his camera.

"This has to be recorded," he said. Then he opened the gate.

Lillie got out with her camera and took a picture of the car driving through the gate. Then another one with Callan sitting on the bonnet of the car. Then one of them both. She put the camera on the ground, adjusting its height with a small stone, then pushing the self-exposure button.

"Pictures to show that we made it," she said.

Little did they know that there was still a long way to go before they would reach the homestead.

Koonamore Station was like a small bump on the flat landscape. The buildings spread out as if they did not like each other. In the middle a very tall tank-stand. It threw a long shadow; the day was coming to its end. There was no vegetation, only a few old peppercorn trees. A pile of tumbleweeds, caught by the iron bars of the tank-stand, had been stopped on their journey into the flat country. Lillie felt like an alien in this environment.

A tall, lean man with a very large hat came up to them. He kept his head bent forward to shade his eyes from the low sun. Slowly he walked up to Callan and gave him a friendly slap on the back.

"How are you, mate? Saw you comin' from a long way off. All that dust gave you away. Yes, she is a dry country. Haven't had any rain in years. So, you made it, mate! Good on you!"

Callan introduced Bill, who ran his eyes over her. She felt scrutinised. It made her feel very uncomfortable.

"So, this is the little lady you told me about?" He nodded and touched the rim of his hat. "I'll show you to your lodgings, mate, follow me. Take the car. Nothing is close here. Mind if I jump in?"

He slid into the backseat of the Dodge, only to be confronted by Tom who hissed.

"Jeez! What have we got here?"

Tom jumped onto the back window and made himself as flat as he could.

They stopped outside a very old, dilapidated stone building. It had a roof and a door, but no glass in the window. Most of the floorboards had been eaten by white ants. There was a small fireplace.

"Cosy," said Callan. "Does the fireplace work? Can we light a fire?"

"Yeah, I'll get you some wood. It's a bit scarce here. You'll need it. The nights are very cold. Sorry, no ensuite or bed. But at least you got a roof over your head. Also, can't invite you for a meal. The cook is not at all accommodating. Actually, she is a grumpy hag. Doesn't like visitors from the city. But do come and join us later. The shack there on that little hill, that's where the station hands live. I'll see if I can talk cook into getting you some breakfast. We eat at 5.30 am sharp. Tomorrow we'll be off rounding up and marking lambs. Anyway, see you later for a cuppa? No alcohol on these premises!"

Lillie made the place as comfortable as she could. Callan lit a fire. Tom stayed in the car, the door left open for him to be able to get out when he felt brave enough to do so. Soon the shabby room was shrouded in darkness. The fire threw its flickering glow around making the place look quite cosy. They cooked a simple meal and then wandered up to the 'house on the small hill'. The ground was as dry as dry. Vegetation crunched under their shoes like cornflakes. The night was clear and bitterly cold.

Arriving at the old stone building they could, even in the dark, see the neglected state of the station-hands' quarter. The entrance door took them straight inside the common room. It had a large fireplace, with a hole in the bottom of the chimney. A tree trunk was fed through it into the embers. Chairs had been placed close to the hardly visible flames. In the embers a blackened billy can. The room was freezing. There were four chairs, all occupied by rugged-up men. One of them had a brown kelpie dog lying next to him. The dog lifted its head as it heard Callan and Lillie enter the room. Bill got up to greet them.

"Grab a chair, come and sit by the fire. If you can call it a fire."

Lillie found a chair. She had to walk past the dog. He growled and looked at her with his amber eyes.

"What a beautiful dog," she said to the rather rough-looking man.

"Watch, he bites. He don't like women," the man said, lifting his head, showing Lillie a very dark, moustached face. A cigarette stub was stuck to his lower lip. The moustache had a hole burned in it. His hair was thin and badly cut. Putting his dark, rough hands gently on the dog he lowered his face, making Lillie aware that this was the end of the conversation.

"Let me introduce my mate from the city and his girlfriend," Bill said, making room for them by the fire. "Well, Callan I have known for some years now. He and I had the same boss in Melbourne. I used to drive a truck for Mr. Nettlebeck, bringing eggs from S.A. to Victoria, where the dumb-as government had brought in a law about free-range eggs. They said free-range eggs were a danger to the public. So, Mr. Nettlebeck imported them from SA where they did not have such a law. Never managed to find out how he got away with it. Callan worked in the grading factory and in our free time we used to have grouse jamming sessions. He is an ace on the fiddle. You know, he lived in a caravan. So as not to hit the ceiling with his bow he held his fiddle on his chest. Looks real great, I tell you! The little lady Callan will have to introduce."

"This is Lillie", Callan said, no more no less.

They all looked at her. Lillie blushed.

"Now to us," Bill continued. "This old fellow is Charlie, with his dog, Red. That quiet guy we just call, 'Hello You'; he doesn't talk much. That young fellow's name is Tony. He's from the Old Country. Callan, you can probably understand what he says. He's our boss-man."

They sat for a while by the fire, conversation non-existent. Slowly the men got up, placed their chairs by a table and disappeared into some rooms along one of the walls. Bill turned to them.

"Better hit the cot. Early up tomorrow. Managed to talk cook into giving you breakfast. I'll come and knock you up. Good night." Pointing at the one miserable globe hanging from the ceiling Bill asked them to turn off the light when leaving. He picked up his chair and put it away, then disappeared into the dark of the room. They heard a door open and close.

Callan mumbled, "These men look like they came from an old people's home. How could they run a sheep station? And that young English boss-man?"

"Maybe there are some more people in the house?" Lillie said as they were finding their way back to their home for the night.

They stoked the fire and turned in. Long did Lilly stare into the dancing flames of their small fire. The day's happenings floating around her. After turning off the highway it felt like they were travelling into an unreal world. Everything seemed to be in decline. Everything was dead and dry, dusty and hot. Even the people here at this place seemed to be half dead. Her head was full of questions. Why would anyone want to live here? How could sheep survive in such a dry place? Slowly sleep took over Lillie's tired mind. Tom had crept into her sleeping bag and was gently purring.

At 5.30 am in the morning Bill came and took them to the homestead. The cold morning air was filled with the drone of a generator. A strong light helped them find the way.

Bill led them across a large area of seemingly dead kikuyu lawn towards the once grand homestead. The building was enclosed by a one-meter-high solid wall. Next to some steps, which helped them get over the wall, was a boat securely tied to a large iron ring. Lillie asked why there was a boat and was the wall there for protection against wild animals? Bill laughed and explained that when eventually the rains come, it usually came in such amounts that the flat land flooded. Then they needed a boat to get from building to building. The wall stopped the water from flooding the homestead.

"Here we are either up to our necks in dust or in mud," Bill said as he opened the door for them.

The kitchen was large, and comfortably warm. In the middle a solid-wooden scrubbed table which could have seated over ten people. Breakfast was served by a bad-tempered woman. She slapped four slices of thin white toast, some crunchy rashes of bacon and two very rubbery, over-cooked poached eggs on a tin plate and put them in front of Lillie. Next to a bowl of toast was a tin of jam and a tub of margarine. A large pot of tea stood in the middle of the table. Next to it a chipped ceramic sugar-bowl and a jug of milk. No one spoke. Thinking of the breakfast table, laden with hunks of bacon, thick slices of brown bread and a big mug of sweet milk-coffee Lillie shared in Austria with Tyrolean farmers before their work made her wonder how these men could go to work on such a miserable meal.

The sun was just throwing a red-yellow glow over the horizon when they took off to one of the holding pens. The dry, icy air bit into Lillie's chest. Wrapped in Callan's old, woollen jacket she went to face this typical June morning in the Australian outback. They followed the old tray-truck which could only be partially seen in the cloud of dust.

One would have never imagined that anything alive could exist in this country. It was bare of all vegetation. The old timber of the holding pens showed up on the horizon as dark lines. She could hear the sheep. As they approached the animals spooked and turned the enclosure into a cloud of dust. The men went to work.

"Keep out of the way, will you," said the young overseer. "This is specialised work! And the lady might not like to be there when we castrate the rams!"

With cameras in hand Callan and Lillie were amongst the workers, always careful to keep out of their way. They recorded the rounding up of the lambs, the sorting of the rams. They photographed when the lambs got their ears marked and then Lillie got a great shot of the overseer biting the testicles off a ram, and then another one. She did not faint.

Then it was morning-teatime. Everyone looked at Lillie.

"Charlie, take the lady and make us a cuppa. Firewood is on the truck," commanded the boss-man from Birmingham.

Charlie lit a fire, put the billy on, lay down on the ground, pulled his hat over his face, and left the rest to Lillie. On the truck was a large tin box. Yes, she found the tea and there was a sort of cake in cellophane wrapping, cups, sugar and powdered milk, also a can of water. No cups for Callan and her. She got their tin mugs out of the car. A good handful of tea into the boiling billy and then swing it around in a circle. Callan had shown her how to make billy tea.

"Tea's on", Lillie called.

Charlie had one eye on her all the time. He'd first hoped she'd faint when they castrated the rams. Then he hoped that the lady from the city would not be able to make a proper cup of tea. He was mistaken. She had shown them that 'ladies' from the city can manage country life. They all enjoyed their cuppa and Sarah Lee's fluffy sponge cake. Then back to work. No word was spoken; only shouts to move the sheep on. Bill ran and managed to catch two lambs, one under each arm. Click, Lillie got him. Bill sat on top of the fence, smoking. Click, Lillie got him; the glow of the cigarette showing. She took photos of the lambs all tight together; all looking at her as if they were waiting for her to make a speech.

Amazed, Lillie watched how these slow old men could suddenly run, chasing down the lambs. How strong they were at grabbing grown sheep, tossing them out of the way, then chase after the lambs. At the end of the day's work they slowly ambled to the truck. The light was starting to go; the shadows almost disappearing. It was time to get back to the homestead.

When entering the workers' quarters that evening, Lillie noticed Charlie with one of his boots off, the bare foot on the table and a plaited-leather belt hooked on his big toe. He was plaiting a belt made from many different coloured leather straps. He sat close to the door, making quite sure Lillie would notice him and she did.

"This is beautiful. Did you make this? Oh, how clever. I am hopeless at plaiting anything. May I touch it?" Lillie reached out to touch the belt.

Saying nothing, Charlie let her finger the belt, then hooked it off his foot and laid it on the table. He had managed to get her attention. He put his sock and boot on, stood up, and without saying anything disappeared into one of the small rooms, the dog at his heels. When he reappeared, he carried two saddlebags, a rug and a whip. He put them all on the table and looked at Lillie, the dog next to him. Not a word from Charlie. She put her hand towards the dog. Not a word. The dog started licking her hand and Charlie spoke.

"I grew up in these parts. I got some pictures. It looks like you like taking pictures."

He produced a small tin from his saddlebag. It was tied with a thin leather strap. A small pile of old photographs spilled on the table.

"That's me, the one on the 'orse, in front of the Waukaringa pub before I'd gone to war. You know, the big one. That there's me mum. She wasn't happy at me joinin' the army. You see there wasn't nothin' going on in Waukaringa. And there's me as a boy. And …"

Lillie was looking at the buildings of the town they had just come through. Now a dead town; not too long ago this man's home.

"What happened to Waukaringa?" she asked

"The gold run out. The men got jobs as roustabouts. A lot left. Some took their 'ouses with 'em. Some said they'd come back. But never did. Some died there. There's still one old bloke livin' there. He'll die there. Poor bugger's sick."

"What happened to the pub? It seems to have been quite a grand building."

"The publican carried on 'til he got too old and then he sold the joint. It was bought by a half-caste. The men didn't like him. They wrecked the place. Stupid thing. We lost our pub. Now we gotta go to Yunta. This station's dry, no booze here."

He was playing with his whip as Lillie thumbed through Charlie's life — all kept neatly in a tin tied up with some leather strap. Oh, how she wished she could have some of the photos. She loved old photos with great passion; so much history hiding in any one of them. Still, she got an insight into this strange man's life and into the town of Waukaringa.

"Do you still use horses for rounding up sheep? Do they still have horses on this property?"

Lillie had only seen motorbikes when looking about the buildings of the homestead.

"Yeah, they still 'ave 'orses, I like'em better'n motorbikes. 'Orses just trot along. Got to steer motorbikes. I hate motorbikes. 'Orses seem to know what ya want. Motorbikes are 'ard work and bloody noisy. Sorry for sayin' bloody."

"Any chance of getting some shots of you lads on the horses?"

"You'd 'ave to ask that young boss-man."

The next morning the landscape was shrouded in fog. The desolated surrounds had disappeared. The stage was set for the men with their horses waiting to have their photos taken. Charlie sat on his horse as straight as a young man. It looked like he had trimmed his moustache. The two saddlebags were placed behind the saddle. The dog sat on a rug in front of Charlie, who was looking down on Lillie. The beautifully crafted whip was draped over the knob on the saddle. The old man's face was black from the shade of the battered hat. She had to get some light into his face. But she did not want to lose the backdrop of an old fence and the drooping branches of the peppercorn tree. Nor did she want to change the atmosphere and Charlie's mood. The fog had wiped out everything else around them.

"Could you look out into the distance?" Lillie asked, hoping to get some light onto his face.

He lifted his head and looked out into the fog. Click, click. She managed to get the face, then Charlie with his dog, and then a picture of the two with the horse. Then the fog lifted, and the distant landscape reappeared, the atmosphere changed.

Bill's horse was far too small for him. They all laughed as he put his long legs around its neck. The young manager, dressed in a sort-of cowboy outfit, rode a beautiful sandy-coloured horse. He showed how good a rider he was. They took some shots of him too. Then the young manager from Birmingham gave the men the morning off.

Bill, Callan and Lillie wandered up to the 'house on the hill'. They stoked the fire and Bill made tea. Later the manager joined them. He told Callan about his life in England and how he got the manager's job here in the outback.

"By fibbing," he said with a laugh.

"What is fibbing?" Lillie asked.

"It is sort of telling tales, sort of lying," Callan explained.

"This place is easy to run. Easier then manoeuvring a bus through the streets of

Birmingham, I tell you."

Bill had brought an old map and put it on the table.

"Here," he said. "The map of Koonamore. We are here, just a little dot. The homestead was first built in 1860-something, renovated in 1940-something and since then nothing has been done to the joint; and you can see it. The only workers the owner — who by the way lives in Adelaide — can get are either old or just out of prison or …" he lowered his voice "… or from Birmingham, England. Mate, I tell you this place is a mess. I am about the only one who knows how to fix a windmill, and I'm getting too old to climb up on one of them things. As soon as I get a bit of cash together, I'm out of here!"

Putting the billy into the fire for yet another cup of tea, Bill went on and on complaining. 'So much tea!' Lillie thought as her bladder was filling up. She whispered into Callan's ear if he could find out where the little place was.

"Where's the dunny, mate?" Callan asked Bill.

"We just go outside. You see the heat and all that quickly gets rid of, you know what I mean."

Callan pointed at Lillie.

"Oh sorry, I see, mate," said Bill. He indicated, "Over there is the dunny. Through that door."

He opened the door and pointed.

"The dunny."

Halfway there Lillie heard Bill calling, but she did not understand what he was saying. Then there was someone running after her.

'Oh no,' she thought. 'My turn first!' She ran as fast as her full bladder allowed.

"Cooee, Cooee. Lillie. Stop. Cooee!"

She opened the door and was confronted by spider webs. No time to panic. Oh my God, all that tea! Next to the hole of the dunny seat, which had a rather beautifully crafted lid, was a hand brush.

'Strange,' she thought. 'I wonder what you do with that.'

When she stepped outside, Bill and Callan looked at her sharply.

"Are you OK?"

"Why shouldn't I be? What is the meaning of the brush? I did clean the seat before sitting down."

Bill looked at the ground in embarrassment. He would never swear in front of a 'lady'. Talking about toilet matters was just not on.

"Well, the brush is used to brush away the red-back spiders from UNDER the seat. They like to live in dark, damp places. They can bite, when you — well, you know what I mean. You see, we never use the dunny."

On the way back Bill told them red-back spider stories and made

Lillie aware of the dangerous animals in Australia. From then on, her eyes and ears were always searching for dangers lurking in the undergrowth.

The rest of the day Lillie spent looking around the buildings. She came across an old blacksmith's shed. It was a beautiful solid-stone building. All the tools were in their allotted places. The forge had not been used in years.

"They ain't fixin' things here no more."

Charlie startled her.

"It all gets flown in from Adelaide. What's broke stays broke; shame, somehow. Me dad fixed everythin'. He showed me how fix'n things, but no one fixes things no more."

"It is a beautiful workshop."

"Yeah, but good for nothin'. It'll disappear. Like all things do."

He walked slowly out the doorway, back into the desolate surrounds of the place. Lillie followed him — looking into the dusty, dry landscape. The large tank-stand on its high legs in the middle of the sad buildings; the tumbleweed piled up against its metal legs.

"We're 'aving a drought. It 'asn't rained forever. Kids six years'n under aven't seen it rain. They're truckin' the sheep down south. Here there's only the breedin' stock left. If we don't get rain, they will probably carc it"

He lit his cigarette stub, singeing his moustache.

"That's why there's only us cripples workin' here. And that bl … Pommy guy. Hardly gett'n any wages. Well, mustn't complain, eh? Got a roof over me 'ead, and tucker in me belly. Dog's happy; he's a good mate."

He patted the dog. He had not spoken so many words for a long time. In a shy gesture he pulled the belt he platted out of his pocket.

"Thought you'd like it."

With that he turned and Charlie in his dusty clothes walked into the dusty landscape.

"Hey Charlie, would you like me to send you some photos of you on the horse? You can then put it with your other pictures. Thanks for the belt. I'll treasure it forever."

He slightly lifted an arm, grunted something, and disappeared into a building, followed by his trusty dog.

Slowly, her head full of thoughts of this dry land, she walked up the hill to the station-hands quarters. Bill and Callan were still talking about the past and the fun they had. She let them talk. She was in her own world — thinking of a six-year-old child not having seen rain; of this huge property yielding nothing; of the sheep she saw having to live on nothing. What did they eat? What a place. An alien landscape; dry, huge, unforgiving. She felt it could swallow her up in a cloud of dust; never to be found again, never to be seen again. Yet this desolate land seized her emotions. It had grabbed her. She felt scared.

"Penny for your thoughts?" Callan said and put his arm around her. He made her feel good and safe and loved. He made her feel alive. He gave her a reason to think of a purposed-filled future.

"I want to go back to Melbourne," she said, and told him what Charlie had talked to her about. "This place is making me sad."

That night in the shearers' quarters, in this desolate, dying place, Lillie lay close to the small fireplace to keep warm. She was overwhelmed with sadness when thinking of the dry land and dying sheep and children who had never seen rain. Burying her head into her pillow she quietly started to cry. All her mind could see was death. Was that going to be her introduction to the 'Outback'? Callan put his arms around her and held her tight.

That night in the shearer's quarters in this dying place they created a new life.

BOX FOUR

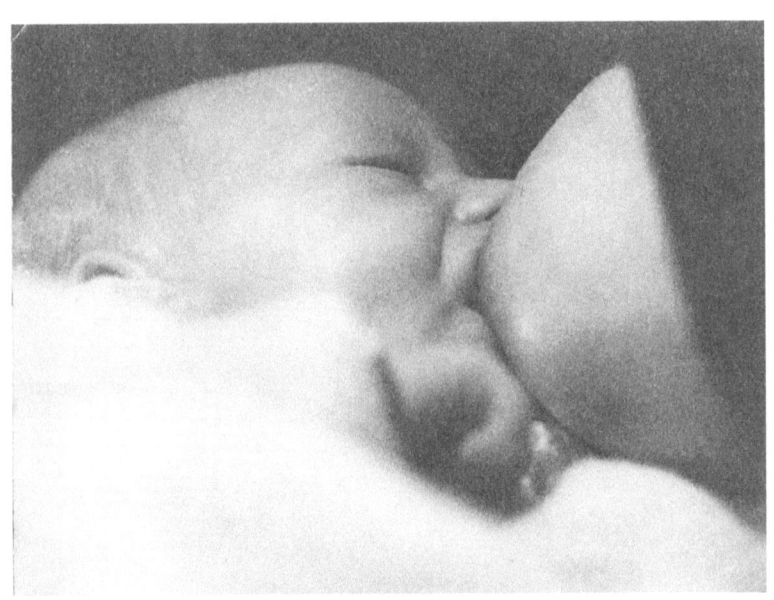

Callan's steady hand had marked it with a thick, black texta. NO.3 CHILDREN. She closes her eyes. Tears well up again. She can almost smell the sweet scent of her firstborn. Feel the soft skin of the baby. She remembers, Oh, how she remembers, the feeling of great wonder at having given birth to a little person.

Lillie leans back and lets her mind wander to her three children, now grown up with children of their own. She will not need to open this box. All the images were burned into her mind.

A LIFE UNPLANNED

A tight-bound little bundle was handed to Lillie. The small screwed-up face, looking out of the firmly wrapped parcel, squinted at her.

"Your son," the nurse said, with a very well-practiced smile. "Isn't he gorgeous? What are you going to call him?"

After having placed the little parcel in Lillie's care, the nurse left to attend to her many other duties on the ward.

'It is so tiny', Lillie thought, as she started unwrapping the baby. A perfect little body stretched out on her lap. Ten perfect tiny toes; chubby legs. He stretched his little arms with ten perfect little fingers. Then he produced a big yawn, a little noise escaped. She gently pulled the rug over the tiny creature and held him.

'My boy, our creation!'

It was the fourth day of the fourth month, 1966.

"What do you think you are doing!?" The nurse harshly pulled her out of her blissful feeling. "He needs to be rugged up tight!" And she took the baby and swaddled it up into a cocoon again.

Lillie knew nothing about babies. There was very little time to find out about babies. There was little time to learn. She had been at work the nine months she carried this child. It was now Monday, early afternoon. On Friday she was still training the new photographer who was going to take over her job. For almost two weeks he had been with her, full of questions. Oh, how she wished the child would arrive. And now, when it had, it was taken away again by the nurse. She suddenly felt cold and alone. Callan should be with her! Sliding back into her bed she started to doze.

How her life had changed.

After she discovered that she had a new life growing within her it became just that; a new life, a new life for her and Callan. Not the life they had imagined. But can one plan a life? They got married at the registry office, a grey, unromantic building from the 19th century. Brother Axel was best man. Her friend, Melita from work, bridesmaid. 'Grandad', Ruth's father, was there as well. It was a simple ceremony. The man sitting behind a large desk pointed at a document. 'Sign here, here and here', and with that their reunion was recorded; for better or for worse. The man smiled, settled back in his chair and thanked them. Outside the door the next couple was waiting. It was a large group of people. The bride in a flowing white dress, holding a bunch of white flowers. Behind her were several bridesmaids, the groom, and an entourage of family.

Lillie wore her 'Dirndl'. On her mother's insistence Lillie had brought her Austrian national costume with her.

"Never know, when you can use it!"

Melita also happened to have kept hers. They both looked splendid in their birth country's national dresses. To include her Norwegian ancestry, Lillie decided to fasten the top of her blouse with an old ornate Norwegian silver clasp. Callan wore a suit he got on his eighteenth birthday, with a newly bought white shirt and a thin, knitted brown tie. They certainly created a very different picture to the couple that were married after them. But then, are wedding ceremonies not mainly a showing off to the family members and friends? In Vienna Lillie had photographed many weddings. All of them full of pomp and glamour. Most of them in one of the beautiful old churches, the elegance of the bride trying to compete with the captivating baroque ornamentation of the building.

The simple wedding feast was very jolly. On the back veranda stood a long trestle table covered with a crisp white sheet. Salads of all sorts, a roasted chicken and leg of roasted lamb, potatoes and Callan's beloved mint sauce covered every bit of the carefully ironed sheet. Ruth had made a proper wedding cake with icing and writing on it. Lillie thought it was splendid. They created a festive atmosphere, surrounded by the devastated landscape of a newly developed outer suburb, the Australian blue sky above them. The thoughts amongst the family members on this, the 16th October 1965, was charged with emotion, love and expectations for the times ahead. The wedding presents were simple, but practical. In the driveway stood a newly made double bed, on top of it a mattress wrapped in plastic. It was a present from Axel and Ruth. Axel had made the bed, working away in the driveway of the house. Grandad gave them ten pounds as a wedding present. With it they had their honeymoon camping somewhere on the mighty Murray River. Lillie's expectations were too high when she learnt about the longest river in Australia. She imagined the river to be as wide as the Danube back in her home country. Tom, of course, came with them.

She wondered how Tom the cat would react to the newcomer, her son. Would he be jealous? She had heard so many stories about cats and babies.

At the flat in Carmyle Avenue, the wicker basket, with its yellow check lining, was ready for the arrival of the new family member. In the basket, happy as can be, lay Tom, black and fat. Callan was furious; his language foul as he picked the cat up by his scruff and threw him out on the balcony. He wanted everything to be just so right for the arrival of his little family.

"No harm done," said Lillie and shook out the little blanket while Callan cuddled the baby. She unwrapped her boy and put him just in his nappy and tiny singlet in the basket. He started kicking and waving his arms about. One could see how he enjoyed having his limbs freed from the tightly bound little blanket.

The matron, when they left the hospital, presented her with an exhausting number of rules. It was important, she said, to get the child used to a strictly formulated pattern. The boy did not want to fit into this pattern. He created his own routine. The joy of his dad playing with him after their evening meal delighted the baby and soon the night sessions became a habit. After a change and a feed, he would sleep until nine the next morning. The little family worked out their own rhythm in their new life.

Lillie and Callan started to make plans to build a small house on their land in Warrandyte. Bill had finished his job at the Koonamore Station and offered to help by clearing and fencing the house site. Every weekend the small family would travel to the 17-acre block, erect their tents, and set to work. The trees were chopped down and debarked, then cut up for fence posts. Some friends came to help digging the foundations for their small dwelling. Lillie and little Stuart stayed out of the activities, listening to the sound of the axes, the cry 'timber' and the crashing of the trees. Later Callan would teach Lillie how to handle a long saw, a monster of a saw with wooden handles at each end. Bill holding Stuart would chant:

"Lillie, pull, not push. And pull, and pull. Yes, very good."

He would bounce little Stuart, who squealed with joy, to the rhythm of the workers.

The summer came and work slowed. Lillie and the baby did not come along. Then the most horrendous happened. The land between Eltham and Warrandyte went up in flames and with it their beautiful land they had called 'Katandra', the song of birds. When they were allowed to drive up to Katandra they were greeted by a blackened landscape. Lillie had known every tree; she had talked to them all. She had shown them all to Stuart.

Bill tried to convince her, that it all would grow back and look as new. The birds would return and sing again. Lillie just hung on to her boy and shook her head.

"It will never be the same and when will the next fire come?"

The next big blow was the announcement by the landlord that Carmyle House was on the market. They would have to find a new place.

It seemed that the whole of Melbourne was on the lookout for somewhere to live. The house they eventually manage to rent was opposite a railway line and on a bus route. Every bus and train made the place vibrate. A symphony of rattles and tinkles soon taught Lillie to make sure none of the glasses and pans would touch when placed in the cupboards. It was a semi-detached brick house with a long corridor with rooms to the left, creating a feeling of living in a railway-carriage. The kitchen and bathroom at the end with a door leading to the large backyard covered in high grass with a narrow path to a rotary clothes line. At the back door they found old syringes and other rubbish. It was the most untidy, shabby, run-down, disgusting place Lillie had ever seen. Next door lived the Italian landlord and his family. With his 10-year-old grandson as translator, he proudly made them aware of the newly built kitchen and bathroom. It could not have been that new, it was riddled with white ants! But it was a roof over their heads, and it was cheap. Soon they turned the place into a home. Their new abode was situated in Station Street, Box Hill an outer suburb of Melbourne. That was all they could afford.

In the morning the men from next door used to file out, with Mama standing outside handing them their lunch packets. Mama next door then did the cleaning to the music of Dean Martin, singing with all her Italian might. She had the unfortunate habit of throwing rubbish over the fence. Once a shoe came flying, almost hitting Lillie as she hung up Stuart's endless nappies. Angrily, the shoe was hurled back. Mama from next door got the message. That was the end of the rubbish throwing. After Papa came home the music stopped. Papa worked until dark in the vegetable garden, which covered the whole backyard. At the very end of the garden was a pen with a pig and some hens.

On the other side of their 'Casa Prima' lived a very bad-tempered old man. He had the whole backyard covered in large leaves. Every day he closely inspected the plants by parting the leaves, then patting something with a satisfying grunt. It seemed to be some sort of a vine. The plant also ventured into their messy backyard. When she examined the plant, the neighbour called out, warning Lillie to leave his precious plants alone.

"What sort of fruit grows on those vines with the big leaves?" she asked Callan

"They are pumpkins. You know the yellow mash they serve you in pubs. Why?"

Callan was stressed. His new job was getting him down. He was not cut out to work as a linesman for the Electricity Commission. He needed to find another job. He needed to find a better house for his family! Every Saturday they had been looking. On top of all that, Melbourne was sweltering in a heatwave, and on top of that, Lillie was expecting another child. He felt inadequate. He felt that he had let-down his little family. He felt that life would continue like that forever.

To Lillie the white weatherboard house sitting on a slight rise above the quiet street was exactly the kind of place where she could bring her new child. The front of the property was terraced. A number of large silver birches grew there. It reminded her of Norway and the wonderful time she spent there. Walking up the stone steps from the street they entered the house. All the rooms were large, light and inviting, including the kitchen, which doubled as a dining room. At the back part was a sizeable sunroom looking out into the yard, tidy and private. The house was partially furnished.

"I love it," she said to the agent.

'We can't afford the rent,' thought Callan.

He saw the excitement in Lillie's face as she stood amongst the silver birches holding her large belly. He smiled at the agent.

"We'll take it."

No. 10 Palmerston Street, Camberwell activated a new chapter in Lillie's life.

Little Jane arrived in the afternoon of the 8th of April 1967, again a baby in a great hurry to be born. When Lillie unwrapped the bundle, the nurse had handed her, the most beautiful little creature looked at her. Her first child had been short and stocky, no neck at all, and a screwed-up little face. This baby was long and thin, with long straight limbs. On its neck a perfect little face. Yet, Jane was a difficult, determined little thing. Her constant crying made Lillie seek help, but there seemed to be absolutely nothing the matter with the child. She was told some babies sometimes cry to get attention, not to worry too much it will all come to an end. And so, it eventually did. The little family settled down.

Callan found a new job with one of Melbourne's top photographers. He was totally engrossed and happy.

The opposite happened to Lillie. She had become what she never wanted to be: a housewife. She felt that she spent her life making lunch for her husband, kissing him 'goodbye' in the morning; all day at home with her two small children, then dinner. In the evening a tired husband, Friday shopping. The wheel of boredom went around and around.

Knitting seemed to break up the monotony. First a jumper for her brother, with a simple Fairisle pattern, then she designed a more complicated one for Callan. The owner of the wool shop, a roundish-looking, motherly lady, was intrigued by Lillie's multicoloured choices of wool and wanted to know what she was creating. After having seen one of the jumpers, she invited Lillie to knit a garment to be sold in her shop. The jumper sold. So, Lillie spent all her time when the children were quietly playing or sleeping, counting the stitches of her patterns. Click, click, click went the needles. Count, count, count went Lillie, until one evening Callan got fed-up with the clicking and counting.

"It gives me something to do!" Lillie yelled. "I am bored doing nothing!" And she let go of all her pennt-up frustration.

Had she not tried to get private work taking photos of children?

Had she not put-up posters for wedding photographs? What good was the darkroom with no work? How could she do much at all with two small children? And then he had the car! Also, the knitting brought in some extra cash — which they needed.

"I am bored!" she shouted at the world. "I have turned into the person I never wanted to be! A good housebound wife and mother in a land without friends and family!".

BOX FIVE

Pressing the box tight onto her chest she lets the tears run freely. How he must have felt her frustration. Her unhappiness in her unfulfilled life. And how it must have hurt him not knowing how to help. He did eventually come up with an answer. Never could he have guessed how this small thought of goodwill would change their life.

She opens the lid. On the top an image of her first pottery studio in the garage of their rented house in Palmerston Street, Camberwell, Melbourne.

CIRCUMSTANCES

Callan could see Lillie's despair, how she was unfulfilled and therefore deeply unhappy. Remembering her excited stories from her Norwegian uncle's pottery studio, Callan decided to enroll Lillie at the local Technical School where pottery night classes were being held. Unfortunately, the last place had just been filled. Not to be beaten he then looked for a place where he could hire a pottery wheel. At the Potters Workshop Callan managed to find everything Lillie would need to start her pottery venture. Over the weekend he turned the garage into a studio. Lillie was ecstatic. Her joyful singing and dancing made Tom the cat flee onto the roof of the garage.

Touching the clay, savouring its earthy smell, took Lillie back to her very young years when she had visited her mother's homeland, Norway, for the first time. It was in 1952. With Europe cut up by the occupying forces, the train trip from Vienna to Oslo was a long one. Many times, she had to change trains; often she had to show her new passport. Ten-year old Lilli was relieved when the journey came to an end. In Oslo her uncle's pottery studio kindled her love for clay. She watched for hours how the lump of clay — the piece of mud — was turned into a beautiful pot. It was mesmerising to watch the clay being drawn up into a cylinder and then shaped into a cup or a vase. One cup after another, her uncle produced. Soon there was a board of pots, all the same. She was allowed to have a try. With the help of her uncle a little vase slowly turned around on the potter's wheel.

"I want to be a potter," she told her mother.

"Oh darling, that is not a job for a woman," was the reply.

She thought of her mother's remark when trying her luck in turning a lump of clay into some sort of a shape. Would she ever be good enough to become a potter? Was her mother right? Filled with determination Lillie got books from the library to show her how it was done.

"One good pot a day," were Callan's parting words before going to work.

Soon the children lost interest in playing with their toys in the sandpit; they wanted to poke their little fingers into the clay. She had no time for that. The mantra, "One good pot a day!" made Lillie put the pottery wheel and herself into the playpen. The children got some clay to play with, but the spinning of the wheel was so much more interesting. Lillie had her first audience.

Callan was born in the pottery district of England, in the Midlands. Even though he had never made a pot, he was familiar with the process. When he came home from work, he would pour himself a beer, go out in the garage studio, look at Lillie's work, and proceed to cut all the cylindrical pots in half to see how they were made, to see if the thickness from top to bottom was even. Then came the praise and criticism. Until one day the word, "Perfect!"

With an exhilarated feeling of success, Lillie started making different shapes. The first six cups still hang on the dresser in her home. The next step was to get her first useful creations fired. They had become friends with the proprietor, Ken, of 'Potters' Workshop'. Ken introduced them to a potter who would fire the work. He also recommended a supplier of glazes.

The laundry/darkroom was turned into a glazing room. Having always been interested in weighing and mixing, Callan started experimenting in making glazes.

As the shelves in their kitchen filled up with all sorts of household wares, the bank account slowly decreased. Callan was getting worried. Lillie, having now been a potter for three months, decided to hold an exhibition in the front garden, only inviting friends and neighbours. Amongst them were Callan's employer and his wife. Mark Strizick was very happy to see Lillie being engrossed in her work.

"A happy wife makes a happy husband. A happy husband makes a good worker. A good worker is an asset to the employer, namely me." Mark said with a smile as he picked up a large jug. "I like your jugs; they look good and round and in need of being filled up with something cool and refreshing."

He bought the jug. He also offered to help Lillie financially in setting up her studio.

The exhibition was a great success and brought in enough money to buy half a small electric kiln. Mark Strizick gave Lillie a loan for the other half and for the kiln furniture to go with it. All she needed to do now was find out how to pay him back!

She got an idea! Lillie's ideas always worried Callan.

"I am going to teach," she told him. "There must be lots of people out there who were not able to get into a pottery class like me. As long as I do not get someone who knows more than I do! Also, I can keep on learning!"

Callan admired her confidence. He was delighted to see her excited again. Full of life!

Every nerve in Lillie's body was twitching. It was a Tuesday evening. They had an early meal. Lillie could only think about her first class. Five women answered her advertisement in the local paper. Anxiously she walked into the studio. She made sure that everything was to her liking. In the middle of the garage, now her studio, was a sturdy table Callan had built for her. Under it, a bucket of water and a number of packets of clay. On it, sorted out in different containers, tools to be used. Callan had constructed a bench for clay preparation. A packet of opened clay, ready for use, was placed invitingly on it. Trying to settle her nerves, she moved the containers holding the tools from one side of the table to the other, then back into the middle. A knock on the big garage doors made her heart race.

"Are we in the right place for pottery classes?"

Two young women stood outside. Then three more came up the driveway.

"Come in. Come in. Welcome to my studio. Do come in. I am Lillie."

Lillie cut some clay from the packet and put five pieces on the table. She was terrified. 'Here goes,' she thought, and started with her first blunder.

"Any of you ever used clay before?"

Empty faces looked at her. The women shook their heads.

"Oh, good!" Lillie continued. "Well, I feel you should get familiar with the material. Introduce yourself to it. Have a play, feel, and squeeze; see what happens."

Lillie picked up a piece if clay and with swift fingers she turned it into a small creature. Not a good start. The five women looked at her and started poking and squeezing the clay, then turning the strange object this way and that. They looked at their smiling teacher, wondering what sort of education in clay they were going to have. They have come to pottery class to be taught how to make a pot!

Callan saved Lillie. He had put the children to bed and came into the studio to see how everything was going. Immediately he could feel that she was struggling. Having been an art-teacher in England, he knew how to handle students. He smiled at the ladies.

"What about a pinch pot?"

Oh, he could be so charming.

"It is a very ancient way of making a bowl or a cup."

So, they all set out to make a little bowl. Holding their ball of clay in one hand they followed Callan's movements. Slowly and gently, he manoeuvred the clay in his hands, looking and smiling at each of the women as he turned the ball into a bowl. Most of the students ended up with flat dishes. Still, everyone was happy with what they had made.

"One can never have enough ashtrays, Callan," one of the women remarked when proudly looking at her plate-like bowl.

Lillie had learnt her first lesson in how to teach pottery. Her students wanted to make useful objects. They did not just want to have a feel, a poke, as an introductory exercise. They had come to make a pot. Lillie needed their money! With a lot of help from their inexperienced teacher all of the women produced some object or another. They left happy and proud of their efforts.

The phone kept on ringing. Lillie filled Thursday, then Monday. Then she had to learn to say, "Sorry but I am booked out," taking contact numbers in case someone dropped out. She started a children's class on Saturdays. Something she enjoyed immensely. The children's imagination and creativity were boundless. They did not strive for perfection. Just having created something gave them the feeling of satisfaction and great pride.

When the first acceptable works were fired and glazed there was great excitement amongst the students. This was a small triumph in Lillie's new life. On that evening, after the class had finished, and everybody seemed to be happy with their works, Callan and Lillie sat down with a glass of port and celebrated.

———◆———

Lillie's mother, Mai, had arrived from Vienna for a six-month visit. She had come out to Australia to be with her daughter for the birth of her third child. The thought of meeting her mother again made Lillie very nervous. Would she approve of the way they lived their life? The way she brought up the children. Would she like Callan? Often Lillie was told how she would never make a good wife and mother. With her zero interest in cooking and her dislike of housework.

Camberwell, Lillie's mother thought, was the most beautiful place. She loved the house and the garden with its silver birches. But most importantly, she loved Callan, and she enjoyed their way of life. She loved being able to hang clothes out in the sun to dry. She would bury her face in the dry linen to smell the freshness and the sunshine, something a flat dweller from Vienna could never do. Lillie was overjoyed to see her mother slide into their life with ease.

Mai did not only come to Australia to be with her daughter and her son. Her best girlfriend and bridesmaid lived in Melbourne. Liesl had to flee from the Nazis and leave her beloved Vienna, leaving most of her family behind. Mai and Liesl had met at the conservatorium of music in Vienna. The love of music had brought them together. When they met again in Melbourne after all those many years, time just fell away. The past was never mentioned. Only their time together now was of importance. Only the future mattered.

With great emotions Mai looked at her youngest daughter. Not too long ago she had held baby Lillie in her arms. The thought of her youngest child going to give birth to a baby of her own, was overwhelming. She thought of the times when Lillie was born. It was towards the end of the Second World War. Vienna was evacuated, they had to flee from the city to the country. Life and future were uncertain. How happy she was that her children did not have to live in those times. She gave her daughter a hug. "All the best. Now, you just go! Don't worry about me! I will look after the children. I know what to do! After all, I have had six of them. Just go! Drive carefully!" and she started to walk up and down the hallway. "What shall I cook for you, Callan? What do you like? Do you need a clean shirt for work?"

He gave her a big hug. "I will be fine. I just need a cup of tea in the morning, strong with a dash of milk and one sugar. I will stay at home tomorrow. Just relax."

Liam was a small baby, born just before sunrise. The boy and Lillie lay together in the hospital bed watching the day arrive. They watched each other. He was very alert, looking at his mother with intent. Looking at her as if he was trying to remember something, or maybe just checking her out?

It was the 27th of January, 1970.

During Lillie's hospital stay, Callan had taken over the pottery classes, but as soon as Lillie came home, she was back in the garage studio. Not that there was a lot of work done. Everyone wanted to hold the baby.

The children were fighting in the back of the station wagon. Nursing Liam, Mai tried to entertain them with songs. Callan was on the edge of losing his temper. They were on their way to visit friends in a small town called Maldon. It was the Queen's Birthday long weekend, and the Calder Highway was bumper-to-bumper with holiday-makers. The windscreen wipers could hardly keep up with the rain. It was not a good beginning to a long needed holiday.

After the turn-off to Castlemaine, the road got narrower and very windy. There was hardly any traffic. They continued through Castlemaine and on to Maldon. A simple wooden sign told them that they had arrived at Maldon, Australia's first notable town. Along the road into town tiny weatherboard cottages huddled into the trees.

Slowly, so that he would not miss the turn-off to their destination, Callan drove up the avenue of bare-branched elm trees. Empty shops with 19th-century verandas watched them go by. They turned left, as told by the map their friends had drawn for them. There was a closed shop on the corner. They turned up a slight rise. Warnock House looked most inviting with smoke coming out of both of its chimneys.

In the parlour of the historic house the table had been laid with a delicious lunch. In the grate of the ornate fireplace a roaring fire. The room smelled of old with a whiff of lavender. Every item was from a time long gone; from the furniture to the little ornaments on the mantlepiece. The tableware also was antique. Callan picked up a bowl and turned it over.

"I can tell you are a potter. Yes, it is Spode from the Midlands in England; I think Stoke-on-Trent," Nancy, who had come in from the kitchen with a bowl of salad, looked at Callan. "Aren't you from that part of the world?"

Callan smiled and nodded. He offered to get a bottle of wine to go with their lunch.

"Why not? If you can find one! Country pubs don't stock wine. Beer and spirits, that's what the men here like to drink," was Nancy's answer.

Callan took off to find a pub. Up the road he saw the Kangaroo Hotel, a grand-looking building. The town was empty. The shops looked unoccupied. He walked past the modern fire station and entered the pub.

"G'day," said the barman.

The pub was deserted. Maybe it was too early for the punters? Maybe the rain kept them away?

"You wouldn't have a bottle of red wine?"

"I might."

Reluctantly the barman disappeared down into the cellar.

"There, that's $2."

With a disagreeable grunt he noisily put a very dusty bottle on the bar.

The wine was a great success. So great that Callan decided to get some more for dinner and for the next day. Then who would complain only having to pay $2 for a good bottle of wine?

"How many bottles of that wine have you got?" he asked on his second visit.

Matt, the barman, pushed his face over the counter and slowly hissed, "Blokes — Drink — Beer, mate!". And with that disappeared back down the cellar. Callan bought what he could carry.

Maldon, on that grey, cold, miserable Queen's Birthday long weekend, had completely enchanted Callan. They sat, after a long slow drive home, in their Camberwell kitchen, drinking a glass of fine Maldon wine.

"I do like that little town of Maldon, you know," Callan said, "I could quite easily live there."

"What is so special about Maldon? I did not have much of a chance to see any of it, with the children. Then the weather was not too inviting. And when we were driving, I was busy keeping the children quiet. So, what was so special?" Lillie felt left out.

"The first thing that struck me was the approach to the little town. No ugly suburban houses. It reminded me so much of England the way the town just stopped. None of that ticky-tacky horror of brick veneers! Then wandering up to the pub and into the shopping part of the place, well, there was a sort of sleepy charm. The old houses gave me some sense of history, which I miss so much in this country. Then there was a big white house-cum-shop, right up at the end of the shopping street. I thought I could live there on the top end of the town looking down the street and up to the hill. You know, it could almost be an Australian, 'Under Milkwood'. Yes, I feel I could live there."

"Why don't we?" answered Lillie, who knew how much Callan disliked Melbourne. "We could start a pottery. You could sell your land in Warrandyte. Maybe there are jobs available? Who knows? Why don't we go and visit again? It is not that far. We can do it in a day!

BOX SIX

How fast her life did change. How fast everything changes.

She takes the lid from the next chapter of her life. The smiling face of little Jane sitting in a cardboard box looks at her. She was so frightened of being left behind. The children had packed their toys. There was not much to pack. A cot for Liam, one chair, the old clock, Dante's Trunk and the bed her brother had made for them. Most of their belongings came out of the studio. The pottery equipment had taken up all of the room in the removal van.

Lillie leans back against the trunk and smiles. Where would she be now without this enormous change? Yes, where would she be!

MADNESS OR INTUITION

They often drove up the Calder Highway to see their dream village. During one of their visits to Maldon they stopped off at the nearby, larger town of Castlemaine and visited the Art Gallery. With great excitement the director listened to their plans of opening a pottery studio in the district. She even encouraged them to do so and offered to help them wherever she could.

"We need to find an inexpensive house to rent and then I must find a job."

Callan suddenly felt worried about the decision in pulling up all their roots in Melbourne. A phone call from the curator of the Castlemaine Gallery completely settled Callan's doubts. If he was interested, there would be an opening for an art-teacher at Castlemaine High School the following year. Also, she had found them a cottage. The rent was only $10 a week.

They decided to take the cottage, sight unseen. One could not grumble over the $10 a week rent. They paid for six months. After that they hoped the land in Warrandyte would sell. Then they would be able to buy a house in Maldon. Maybe the white one at the top of the shopping centre?

Friends thought that they had lost their minds, gone bonkers, behaved irresponsibly. With three children and one of them barely one year old, and with no money! To relocate the whole family to a small country town because of its charm and romantic ambience! To just leave a good job! And what about the newly established pottery venture? They threw their arms in the air!

"Really, an Australian, 'Under Milkwood'. You'll be back within the year!" one of them said.

The removal van was loaded to the brim, so was the car and trailer of their friend Allan who offered to help in their transition. He also volunteered to stay with them for a few days, assisting them to settle into their new home.

Carefully, Callan placed his beloved, partially filled tropical fish tank, still accommodating the plants and fish, in the car. He secured it with several household items, hoping to keep it stable. Lillie had their cat Misha with a litter of kittens on her lap. The children were squashed in-between everything. Tom the cat had quietly passed away a few years earlier.

As they drove away from their home of four years, away from the silver birches, away from a settled life, Lillie felt a slight fear rising. She said goodbye to the quiet street. One of the neighbours waved them 'goodbye'. Lillie did not look back and when they got onto the open road and everyone had settled in the car, she dismissed her anxiety and started to look forward to the new life facing her.

Arriving in Castlemaine, after a nerve-wracking drive with whingeing children, restless kittens, and a sloshing fish tank, they dropped by the agent to get a key for their 'Shangri-La'. Felix Cappy took them to their new home: No 11 Saint Street. The little stone cottage was sitting almost at the bottom of the steep property. High grass and weeds surrounded it. A wilderness of a garden! The place looked as if it had not been occupied since the late 19th century.

With screaming and smoking brakes the removal van came down the steep hill. They all watched in horror, wondering if it would be able to stop at all! The driver did manage to turn the van and park it next to the front — or was it the back of the cottage?

After everything was off-loaded, Lillie found some cups, a teapot, tea and sugar, but there was no milk. They all sipped their sweet black tea and talked about the trip up. Then the van drove away, and they were left amongst their few belongings, suddenly realising how uncertain their future was.

Beside the stone cottage was a bungalow, attached to it the bathroom and outdoor toilet. While Lillie and Callan made up some makeshift beds in the stone cottage, their friend Allan moved into the bungalow. The kitchen was a few steps higher than the rest of the house. The roof of the kitchen merged with the hill. The one small window looked out into the wild garden. The kitchen itself was very basic. A wood stove and a very old gas stove; there was a sideboard, table and a few chairs. Most of the plaster from the walls had fallen off and one could see the bare wall made from local sandstone. The door was very narrow, and Lillie wondered how they would be able to get the fridge not only up the old stone steps, but also through the door.

Somehow Lillie managed to rustle something up for dinner. The children were bedded down. Callan got busy with his fish tank. The cat had disappeared with her kittens. As they were relaxing with a glass of wine, celebrating their new life, cheering the future, hoping for the best, the first fish floated to the top of the tank looking very sick. Callan loved his fish. Even as a boy he had fish, in jars and in bottles. When they settled in Melbourne, Callan had lashed out and got a tropical fish tank.

Obviously, the journey did not suit the fish. One after the other, they floated to the surface, flapping a bit, and then they just lay on top of the water: lifeless. It would have been a miracle if they had survived the journey with all that sloshing about. The next day the tank was cleaned out and put aside in a safe place to be restocked at a later date.

The following day, the 25th of January, was Liam's first birthday. A party had to be organised. No time for fish. Not that kind anyway. They found a fish-and-chip shop, and everyone could order what they liked.

Sitting on the veranda at the back of the house, munching away on their special dinner, they realised that the house was facing backwards. Looking at the cottage from this side gave it a rather charming appearance. Maybe the property had been sub-divided? Below them they could see the roof of a modern house, beyond a creek. It seemed that there once was a formal garden. Overgrown remains of a path flanked by dead rose bushes went from the front door in a straight line and ended up in next-door's fence. A circle of up-ended bricks surrounded a now far too big holly tree. The ground was littered with prickly leaves. The cover was so thick that not a weed managed to grow. What did grow there though were a lot of empty cans, beer bottles and other rubbish. It showed the kind of occupancy the cottage had enjoyed. During dinner they planned what to do with the garden. Allan offered to bring some instruments of destruction, as he called the garden tools, when next in Melbourne. But there was never any gardening done. Time was filled with getting on with life.

"Oh dear, where is the iron?" Lillie panicked. "You need a crisp-looking shirt! You are going to a job interview, remember? That's today!"

"Please, relax. We only arrived a few days ago! Just relax," replied Callan.

The iron was found. Lillie looking at him in his suit and crisp shirt, nodded nervously, "Good luck!"

Callan was off to see the headmaster at Castlemaine High School to talk about the position offered to him before they moved. It was a very hot January day. Callan looked nervous and bothered.

"Well, yes, good luck to me."

And off he went up the hill to the car parked on the road.

"We'll celebrate tonight, mate!" Allan called after him.

But there was not going to be a celebration. Callan, with his English Teaching Certificate, could not teach in Australia unless he did a three-month crash course in Melbourne. The headmaster had forgotten to mention it.

"Shit, let's have a celebration to 'What Are We Going To Do Now'!" Callan said.

They had just settled down in the shade, on the stone steps by the kitchen, where they could avoid the hot afternoon sun, when they heard a "Yoo hoo! Yoo hoo!" floating down the hill. Lillie turned around. A tall, thin, elderly lady in a fashionable, soft flowing dress, holding a paper sun umbrella over her head came down the hill.

"Yoo hoo! Anybody home?" Her voice was high, almost like singing.

Callan was not in the mood to have visitors and vanished into the house.

With an outstretched arm she walked towards Lillie and Allan. "I am Mrs. Vellacott. I am sort of your neighbour, Mr. and Mrs. Pennington? I live two houses away over there." She elegantly waved her arm.

Jane was trying to carry screaming Liam. He had somehow got

into the prickly holly bush and wanted his mother.

"Oh, sweet child, this baby is far too big for you to carry. Let me," Mrs. Vellacott offered.

"I heard you are artists," she cast her eyes around, inspecting the place. "How exciting! It's so good to get artists to move into Castlemaine. Please, anything I can do for you. I just live, well, sort-of next door. You must come for tea. Shall we make a time now?" she continued, putting Liam down.

"Any time," Lillie replied, "That is very kind of you. Then you can meet my husband."

"Tomorrow, then, let's say 10.30 am?"

"Thank you, it will be a pleasure"

"Good". Mrs. Vellacott said and turned to ascend the steep hill slowly and elegantly, holding her parasol to shade her head from the sun.

With an angry face Callan raced out of the kitchen.

"What the hell did you do that for? High tea! My God, I left England because of that sort of thing!" he complained.

"We need to meet people and I feel that this lady knows everyone. You don't have to come, if high tea revolts you. I have never experienced high tea."

Not quite sure how to get into the house, they walked down a steep path to what seemed to be the way to the front door. The very large Victorian house surrounded by a well-kept, sizeable garden, was on the corner of Saint Street. It seemed to have a number of entrances. They came to a driveway, which took them to the back of the house. Here they could see the magnificent old stone foundations, which created an open cellar or downstairs dwelling. The stone walls disappeared into the hillside, giving the house an elevated feeling.

"Yoo hoo!" came from above.

Mrs. Vellacott was bending over the wrought-iron balustrade of the veranda, which went around two sides of the building. "You can take the door on the side. Over that way." She pointed back to from where they had come.

Climbing back up the hill they found the door, which led into the most impressive corridor. They had walked into a different time. Everything was Victorian. Having grown up in a modern flat in Vienna, Lillie had never seen anything like it. It was the sameness of style throughout the whole house which made Lillie stop and stare.

"I see you like my house, Mrs. Pennington," she said, approaching them out of the gloom of the dark corridor. "We will have tea on the veranda. There is a cool breeze and a nice view."

Her hand outstretched, she approached Callan. "Mr. Pennington?"

"Oh please, Callan, call me Callan and this is Lillie." Callan replied, taking her hand.

She led them to the veranda, where a cast-iron table and wicker chairs waited for them. On a little side table was a tray of sandwiches and little cakes. It reminded Lillie of the time, when she was a small child, and her grandmother invited her to have a hot chocolate. They drank out of the same delicate cups and used the same little plates for their cakes.

"Sandwich, Lillie?" brought her back from her grandmother's room. A plate of little sandwiches was held in front of her. Callan's questioning look made her talk of her memory.

"Charming," was Mrs. Vellacott's answer. "But let us talk about you. What made you come to stay in Mrs. Green's cottage?"

"Mrs. Green's cottage?" Callan was puzzled. "We are paying Mr. Cappy; he is our landlord."

"Yes, yes. But Mrs. Green used to own it. It has been in her family since the Gold Rush. Several stone cottages were built on this hill. My house was built on top of one of them. One can still see the building. It now looks a bit like a cellar. They were identical little cottages, just that my family became wealthy, the others did not. So, tell me, have you come across the ghost yet?"

Callan and Lillie looked at each other with some excitement.

"A real ghost?" Callan looked at Mrs. Vellacott with expectations.

"Mrs. Green was a good Christian and a kind soul. I knew her well. She was quite old. Her husband had died. Her daughter moved to Melbourne, as all the young people do. I looked after her quite a bit when she was old and sick. Every day I walked across with a bowl of nourishing soup. Her daughter came up when she died. She burned all the manuscripts. Oh, what a shock! They were very valuable!"

She put her cup down with shaking fingers.

"What about the ghost?" Callan reminded her.

"Mrs. Green, as I said, had a big heart. The local reporter and editor of the Castlemaine Mail at that time was a total alcoholic. As nearly all of them are! Most nights the police would scoop him out of the gutter and let him sober up in the cells of the Police Station. Sometimes Mrs. Green would get to him before they did and bring him to her home. He ended up living in the bungalow. In the end the police just brought him, on her request, to her house. He died there and they say he is walking about the place, never actually in the house. Quite a bit around the bungalow and also in the old breezeway, which had been built-in to create a room."

Her manner had changed. The elegant, well-spoken lady had disappeared. She seemed agitated and slightly angry.

"I was away when Mrs. Green died. Her daughter came up and I was too late to save the manuscripts of all the articles published in the Mail since this drunken gentleman started work on the paper.

I saw the smoke coming out of the chimney! Too late! A big chunk of history going up in smoke, all handwritten; worth quite a bit of money."

Mrs. Vellacott angrily moved about in her wicker chair making it creak. She looked over to Mrs. Green's house as if she could see smoke coming out of the chimney. With a long sigh she muttered: "All that history, gone."

Then there was total silence. Even the garden was still. The late cool morning had turned into a hot January day. Lillie looked over the wrought-iron rail through the leaves of the old European trees and on to the town of Castlemaine. She broke the silence.

"I can see the Post Office clock from here," she said.

Mrs. Vellacott's thoughts moved away from manuscripts and Mrs. Green. Gaining her composure, being gracious again, she took Lillie's hand.

"The most important thing now my dear, is to find you a space to set up your studio. Any help you need, just let me know. More tea? Or a cold drink maybe? We still have to eat those little, delicious cakes. I personally think hot tea is best on a hot day."

She got up to make another pot of tea.

"No, thank you" Callan replied, "We'd better be going. Allan is probably sick of looking after the children. Thank you for the interesting story, the tea and everything"

"You are very welcome."

The old Mrs. Vellacott was back, elegant and sweetly charming.

"And do not forget my offer. If you need anything, I am here most days. Also, I do know a lot of people in this town." she called after them.

Aggressive Allan was pushing his mower through the high dry weeds and grass.

"High grass can mean snakes. Snakes and kids don't go together," Stones were thrown, rubbish revealed.

"We need to clear around the house," he continued, whilst pushing the moaning mower through the wilderness. Suddenly, with a loud bang, the machine stopped. The Victa mower had found something. The blades were tangled up in some sort of fabric. Even after removing the problem, all the yanking in the world would not start the motor.

"Just keep the children away from the high grass. And should you need to walk through it, make a lot of stamping noise. That will make snakes run away. Still better: stay away until I get that fixed."

Lillie had never lived in the countryside. First, she found her new life challenging and thrilling. Soon the thrilling feeling disappeared when the challenges became too hard to tackle. The old stone house alone, as charming as it looked, was filled with hard work. With every footstep the plaster would fall from the walls. She decided to remove the lot. Then no one could complain of having gravel in bed.

The kitchen was another trial. The gas stove was quite useless, the wood stove behaved like an enemy. Still, somehow, she managed to put food on their table. And the thought of having a ghost wandering about the house was a little nerve-wracking. Not knowing its whereabouts made trips to the outside toilet a bit daunting.

Lillie decided to get chickens. There was plenty of food for them on the almost one-acre block. Having their own eggs would help stretch the household money. And there was a little shed, ideal for chickens. Lillie bought six hens of the Bantam variety and had a rooster thrown in. The chickens never used the shed to roost. A tree outside the chicken house was much more to their liking. Finding the eggs was a challenge and became the children's job.

Having never had any kind of domestic animals, Lillie needed to learn more about chickens. She wanted them to sleep in the shed, so they could be locked up until they had laid their eggs. That would make life just so much easier. To be educated about chicken husbandry she went back to the Italian lady who sold them to her. Lillie arrived home with a baby goat. Callan was furious.

"She can eat the grass. Allan's Victa mower does not manage this high grass. They were going to kill and eat her, sweet little thing. I will call her Victoria and she will live in the shed. The chickens can stay where they are. Also, one day she will give us milk. She is a Saanen, apparently they are top milk producers."

"Love, Saanen or whatever, nanny-goats must have a baby, just like you did, to produce milk!" a frustrated Callan replied.

So, Victoria came into their life. The first week she just cried and cried. Lillie ended up sleeping with her in the shed, which created a great bond between them. Soon the kid settled down and learnt to be on a chain. Victoria would eat everything and anything she could reach. Grass was not her favourite fare.

The farm grew when Allan came along with six ducklings. They were all called Dinner and Supper. No word from Callan when they took over the children's little paddle pool. He just threw his arms in the air, shook his head and walked away.

A large parcel arrived for Stuart from Vienna. To celebrate his first schoolyear, Mai had sent him a school bag. On the inside she had written his name, Stuart Gunnar Pennington. Proudly he put his new pencil case and lunch into his small backpack and straight after breakfast the whole family walked down to the Castlemaine South Primary School. As the children were shown into their rooms Lillie mingled amongst the parents. Callan talked to the headmaster. Jane was pulling on Lillie's clothes.

"I also want to go to school!" she cried.

"Next year, darling."

"No, not next year, NOW! Everything is next year!" Jane howled.

A woman smiled at her. She seemed to have the same problem with one of her children. Lillie walked over to her and introduced herself.

Mrs. Margaret Harrison was also a stranger in this town, a newcomer, and she was trying to make friends. They owned the Imperial Hotel and the cottage next door to it. Her sister-in-law ran a tearoom in the once grand pub.

"What about a cup of tea?" She asked.

Callan and Lillie had admired the facade of the grand Imperial Hotel and often wondered why it looked closed. They had peered through the windows of the cottage next to it, thinking what a great studio it would make.

Over scones and tea, they discussed the possibility of turning the cottage into a pottery studio. There was just one big problem. The previous tenant almost burned the place down. The floor was badly damaged, and the council had slapped a demolition order on the building. There was absolutely no hope of getting a building permit. Or was there? Allan had been involved with old buildings and felt that they could renovate the inside of the cottage. Maybe then Mrs. Harrison could apply again for a permit. It seemed to be a good plan. Everything was possible. One difficulty was that the offices of the Town Hall were across the road. Building materials had to be brought in at night and stored out of sight. With the renovation plan of the cottage solved, one problem remained. Lillie needed to get her pottery going, to advertise her classes, to make some money. And that as soon as possible.

The small electric kiln, all the clay and glazes and tools, were moved down into the cellars of the old pub. Mrs. Vellacott had given them a very large, old kitchen table. It was great for working on. Soon the cellar looked like a pottery studio.

Life was moving in the right direction. Stuart was happily settled at school; they found a kindergarten for Jane. Margaret Harrison offered to look after Liam. Best of all, the first inquiries for the pottery class started to trickle in.

It looked like the winter rain was never going to stop. At one stage the cellar flooded. Nothing seemed to stop Lillie getting on with her work. Never did she think of the danger she was in with the electric kiln and pottery wheel standing in water. The water problem eventually was solved. The cold set in. There was no heating in the cellar. Wearing beanies, scarves and thick woolly jumpers, Lillie and her three faithful students soldiered on in the bowels of the Imperial Hotel. The winter did not seem to end.

In the cottage, the new studio, Callan and Allan worked tirelessly to be able to get a building permit. Allan, their quiet, stocky friend from Melbourne, became a very important part of the little family. He would load his trailer with building material picked up from secondhand yards and bring them at night into the backyard of the building. During the day the two men would work away, hoping that the council staff across the road did not become suspicious of the noise from the sawing and hammering. Every day was regarded as a success. Soon the place was at a stage where they could confront the building inspector.

Mr. Wynd arrived, clipboard in hand, on the appointed day. Mrs. Harrison, with little Liam on her hip, let him in, stood back and watched as the inspector went over every aspect of the building. Callan and Allan were hiding, listening nervously. Down in the cellar, Lillie could almost feel the tension as she was working away on the pottery wheel. Easter was the deadline for opening the new pottery shop. She heard the door upstairs close. With her hands full of clay, she ran up the stairs to be confronted by three smiling people. Margaret Harrison was waving a form in her hand.

"We got it! The building permit! Let's celebrate!"

They planned on having a grand opening at Easter: only two months away. The shop was taking form; it was looking very respectable with its seagrass matting on the floor, shelves along the walls. The floors had been replaced. The small old kitchen extension, where the fire originally started, repainted. It seemed that the little place had come back to life again.

But the opening was not going to be at Easter.

Again, with clipboard in hand Mr. Wynd arrived. His sheet of paper soon had filled up with all kinds of problems he had found. This happened a number of times. There was no use in arguing. He was the authority; he was the one who gave permission.

Total exasperation had overtaken Lillie. All this work, all the pots she had made. Pennington's Pottery had been officially registered, the document in a frame ready to go on the wall of the new studio. Had she not slaved away in the cold and the wet? Her frustration turned into anger, the anger into a sudden determination.

"I will have an exhibition in the small courtyard; in the cellar," she declared one evening over dinner.

"Absolute madness and a waste of energy. Who will come?"

"We'll see," she replied.

They did come. An article in the Castlemaine Mail made the locals turn up to have a stickybeak at these newcomers. They could check out those hippy folks, and that woman who lived with two men. There was not much going on in Castlemaine in 1971.

Easter came. By Sunday evening Lillie was puffed up with pride. All went extremely well. Lots of sales! And a few more enrolments once they were settled into their new studio. There were inquiries for a children's class. She met and spoke to a lot of locals and felt accepted into their town.

One month later, at long last, the engineer gave them the green light. The framed registration of their business name could at long last be hung on the wall of the studio. All they needed was the public to discover them, to sell the pots that filled the new shelves and to get a few more students.

"We need to get an article in the papers, maybe one of the magazines," Lillie suggested. "What about a Woman's Weekly? I am a working woman, a potter. That should make some sort of an article?"

Callan wrote a press release and mailed it to the Women's Weekly. A reply came. The reporter and her photographer would arrive in Castlemaine on a set day. Panic struck Lillie. It made Callan laugh.

"Well, love, fame at last."

The reporter was an elderly lady with the aura of a school mistress. There was nothing pleasant about her. She reminded Lillie of a teacher from her high-school days in Vienna. The journalist was accompanied by a rather handsome young photographer. He was French and spoke very little English. But then a photographer does not need to speak, just take pictures.

The reporter turned to Lillie and wanted to know if there was a quiet place where they could talk. Maybe a cafe? They went into the pottery where Callan made them all a cup of Pablo Instant Coffee. When handing her the cup he gave her his charming smile.

"That's about all Castlemaine can offer you. Milk, sugar?"

Out came the writing pad and with it a host of questions.

"You see, dear, my magazine is very interested in working women. What you are doing is most intriguing. Now tell me, dear, how do you make a living, how do you survive? Maybe you have a second income? Or some money from your Austrian Family? You have three children, have you not? How do you make ends meet? Surely your artwork cannot sustain you?"

There were questions about their way of living. Not a question about her pottery history. Lillie was proud of how they had managed, how they had arrived at where they were. Then finally a question that made Lillie's anger rise.

"Dear, you would not have some recipes for the readers? It is a woman's magazine, after all."

Callan saw his wife's face turning red. Lillie and cooking never were a great combination. He sent her his beautiful smile. Lillie found herself saying,

"Well, I was born during the war in Vienna. There was very little food to be had. As I told you, my mother was Norwegian, and they love potatoes. My mother could cook 101 different potato meals. I remember quite a lot of them. Yes, we eat a lot of potatoes. If we hit a rabbit with the car, well then there is rabbit as well. And then we have chickens, they give us eggs." She stared defiantly at the reporter who had put the writing pad back in her bag.

The photographer had been walking about taking pictures. He wanted a picture of Lillie at the pottery wheel. With fascination he watched her making a vase.

A few weeks later the article was published. Most of the pictures were out of focus and had been crudely touched up. The emphasis was on her 101 potato recipes. The result of the write-up were letters asking for the recipes. One lady begged to come and live with them. She loved their way of life, had her own caravan, and would be of no bother to them.

"Fame at last!" Annoyed Lillie looked at Callan who quietly laughed. "Maybe we should start a caravan park. The garden is big enough. Find a flat spot and you can stay for free! And I throw a few potato meals in!"

Callan walked up to her and gave her a big hug.

"No one can say that you did not try, my love."

Slowly the pottery became known. Almost every day they had a class of up to six people. They had started to buy the clay by the ton; the little electric kiln was working flat out. Orders were coming in. Lillie had become a production potter.

With an armful of wood and deep in thought Lillie walked into the studio. The Monday class was always a difficult one. The students wanted to make items like teapots, casserole dishes; vessels that needed lots of skill and experience.

A strange man confronted her. He took the logs from her and placed them on the fire.

"My name is Robby Rob, I am a potter amongst other things. I am looking for a job."

They could hardly get by with the money they made! Employ someone?

Lillie looked at him. He was a little older than her; good looking, well spoken, probably English, about as tall as she.

"Sorry, but we can't employ anyone. We don't make enough money as it is!"

"A meal here and there; a drink now and then. I just would like to get my hands into clay again. Make a pot or two for myself. Maybe I can help you this morning? You can see what I can do?"

Callan was out. He had a part-time job as a photographer taking passport and wedding pictures. She did not know what to do.

"OK you can help me this morning. But I cannot make a decision until Callan comes back."

Robbie Rob was extremely good with the ladies. He oozed charm. They liked him. And he was a good teacher. Lillie liked him. There was a sort of wonderful madness about him. After all the tension in her life he felt like a breath of fresh air. Callan agreed to let Robbie join them. They were a good teaching trio. Lillie taught wheel-work, Callan was the glazing expert, and Rob took over the difficult task of hand-building.

The little electric kiln was working flat out. The outside metal cover had rusted and was falling apart. Some of the elements were broken and had to be wired together. Plainly put, the kiln was a danger and dying. A new kiln needed to be bought.

The suggestion by Rob to build a kiln, this time run by gas, appealed to Callan. They ordered kiln bricks. Rob had a potter friend who helped them with planning the design. Burners were bought. The bank balance almost went to zero!

With Rob's draughtsmanship and Allan's experience in building, the kiln went up and was soon ready to be fired. It was to be filled with glazed ware. The door was bricked up and early in the morning the first burner went on. It should take about 10-12 hours to get 'her up' to temperature, which was 1100°C. The tension all day, as one burner after another was lit, was electrifying. Lillie had bought a magnum of champagne. It was in the fridge waiting.

At midnight they shut off the gas and went home. The champagne stayed in the fridge unopened. Callan and Rob spent the rest of the night scheming and planning, drawing, and redesigning. Lillie could hear all sorts of technical jargon coming from their kitchen. Then: "Got it!" When the kiln had cooled down, they offloaded the ware, did some changes to the interior, then all the pots were re-loaded, burner turned on and the whole process of firing began again. This time the champagne flowed. This was a huge step for Pennington's Pottery. They could now take on bigger orders, maybe even find some more wholesale clients.

Slowly swaying to the music, a tall grey-haired, bearded man stood in front of the fireplace in the shop. It was winter. Day after day he arrived to warm himself. His clothes looked well-worn and slightly shabby, but they seemed to be of good quality. A reel-to-reel tape recorder was playing Mozart.

"Excuse me, can I help you?" Lillie asked. She was irritated about him standing day after day in front of the fireplace. He could be keeping customers away. Turning towards her he smiled.

"No, thank you, I just enjoy the music. I used to play the piano. One does not get the opportunity to hear classical music in these parts of the world. Oh, excuse me!", he stretched out his hand. "Rob Sherwin, I live at the back of Barkers Creek." He made a slight bow, turned back to the fire, and again started swaying to the music of Mozart.

Back in the studio Lillie looked at Robby. Pointing towards the shop she asked if he knew this man.

"Rob Sherwin is — was — a local solicitor. He mainly worked on divorce cases. Getting truly sick-and-tired of squabbling couples, he decided to become a dropout. He lives at the back of the old Barkers Creek quarry where he built himself a very illegal stone hut. Watch him, he is a very clever debater and loves a good argument."

"I heard that!" the voice said from the shop. Rob Sherwin walked slowly into the studio. "Well, well, if it is not the charming Robby Rob!"

With an irritated movement Lillie showed them out of the studio.

"Some of us have work to do! Excuse me, I have a class starting soon."

Rob took Robert into the backroom, where they settled down to a chat. Lillie could hear them laugh and argue. It was hard for her to concentrate on her class. As soon as she was free Lillie joined the two men in their conversation. Robert kept on addressing Lillie as 'My German Fraulein'. With irritation Lillie would make him aware that she was not German but Austrian. And so, the argument about those countries started. Lillie enjoyed his impeccable English and loved to argue with him, never getting the upper hand, never winning their dispute. The discussion was ended by Robert saying, "My dear Fraulein, I totally agree with what you are saying. Sorry stringing you along. It is part of my DNA to argue. Maybe, that is why I became a solicitor."

He bowed to take his leave, then walked back to his stone hut in Barkers Creek, leaving Lillie hanging there with her thoughts of the discussion.

They became good friends. Both Callan and Lillie enjoyed his company. He injected interesting subjects into their life of pots and children. Often discussions with Robert would open up new worlds, new directions in their busy life. It made them feel alive again.

The cottage came with an old upright piano. The children loved to bash the worn ivories. When Rob Sherwin found out about the piano, he dearly wanted to play on it. Lillie, having grown up with a grand piano, shuddered at the thought of anyone wanting to use the old instrument.

"As long as I can sit at a piano again, feel it and be able to make some sort of music!" was his reply when Lillie told him about the terrible state of the instrument. Robert was not going to be discouraged.

Almost every day Robert Sherwin would drive to the Saint Street cottage to play, sitting blissfully at the piano swaying to the music of Handel. He seemed to love just one part of 'The Entrance of the

Queen of Sheba'. The poor Queen of Sheba never seemed to enter completely. Rob Sherwin on the other hand used his time in Saint Street to enter both the laundry and bathroom. She thought he looked suddenly very swish and clean. But the house did not have lockable doors. How could they keep him out?

"What if we give him the piano?"

"It is not ours to give away," Callan replied.

Lillie got in contact with the Estate Agent to find out about the piano. Felix Cappy did not know that there was a piano in the house.

"Yes, please, let him have it! That saves me having to take it to the tip!" Felix said with a laugh.

Robert Sherwin was overjoyed. Friends were organised. One had a trailer. Somehow, they got the old instrument out of the house, down the steps, up the hill and onwards to Barkers Creek. That's where things became tricky. Robert's hut was hiding behind a heap of broken slithers of slate. They had to push the rather heavy instrument up and over the small mountain. Many times the piano slid back down, often due to someone starting to laugh. Robert was standing on the top conducting, behaving like some hysterical highbrow pianist keeping an eye on his priceless instrument. There were lots of suggestions on how to manage the move. One suggested, 'Chop the F-thing up.' 'How about rolling it up the hill?' 'Ha!' They managed in the end.

From then on at the Barkers Creek quarry, when standing quietly at the foot of the mountain of slate slithers, one could hear the music of Handel played on a very badly tuned old piano.

Nervously they opened the official-looking envelope from the council. The memory of the difficulties they'd had with the building inspector were still quite fresh in their minds. But the fine-looking letter had nothing to do with the local authority. It was an invitation from the newly formed Castlemaine Traders Association inviting them to be part of their first annual Trades Fair. Would they be interested in demonstrating their craft? Creating a bit of entertainment? Brighten up the static feeling of the stalls? They could use the whole of the stage in the Town Hall.

The stage, which was quite large, was turned into a pottery workshop. Callan built a small kiln, put in a few kiln-shelves and some of their pottery. Robby Rob set himself up in the middle of the stage, where he would hand-build some creation. A very large piece of black plastic was laid on the floor where Lillie was going to demonstrate how to make a vessel on the pottery wheel. Very few people were interested in how a kiln worked. It was the active demonstrations the public enjoyed watching. A crowd gathered around Lillie.

It took her back to the time when she had her first experience in demonstrating her craft in public. It was for the opening of the newly built Doncaster Shopping Centre where the Melbourne Myer store had opened a small, 'All Australian Made Craft Shop'. It was also the first evening of late-night shopping.

The pottery wheel was placed outside the shop. People gathered around. There was no escaping! Terrified, she started. Most people just had a quick look. One lady though kept on watching. She even knelt down to look at the pot from the side and to watch how Lillie's hands drew the clay up. Lillie became agitated and started sweating. Then the woman stood up came to her and asked,

"Where does the clay come from? Are you pulling it out from under the wheel?"

Lillie laughed. She'd thought that an expert was watching her, inspecting her workmanship! Here in Castlemaine people knew her!

It made her nervous and she decided to make safe, simple shapes. Making one pot after another and the shuffle of feet around her put Lillie into some sort of a trance.

Someone gently tapped her on the back. "Can you make anything?" Astounded Lilly turned around. A little boy looked at her.

"Depends, what would you like me to make?"

"A football!"

"I think I should be able to manage that."

And Lillie made the shape of a football. When finished she put it on a small piece of cement-sheet and gave it to the boy.

"How much?" the mother asked, "And how long until it goes hard?"

"No cost. Put it in the sun for a few days. It will get harder, but you still have to be careful with it. You can paint it, if you like."

Before she knew it, there was a string of children wanting her to make shapes for them.

Robby Rob showed the children how they could make their helium balloons float by attaching a small piece of clay to the end of the string. The stage was full of children having a great time. The parents in the meantime could walk from stall to stall, looking at items for sale. Lifting her head, she let her eyes wander over the displays below. The floor was teeming with people. Patient stallholders constantly explaining to the onlooker how wonderful, how useful, their product was; how no one could possibly live without having one. Lillie smiled.

Then a crying child came back. The pot had fallen off the little board.

"Look, it is all squashed!" the child cried

Lillie made her another pot and gave her a lesson in gravity.

"Hold the board straight, then you will not drop your pot."

Then suddenly, "Make me a pot, Mum."

Stuart was standing in front of her. Their friend Allan had brought the children to the Trades Fair. They all held a balloon in one hand, an ice cream in the other.

"What shape would you like?"

"Don't care. I just want it to be BIG!"

"OK. You give me a lick of your ice cream and I make you a big pot and then we all go for a coffee and hot chocolate. I need a break!"

There was no coffee shop in Castlemaine. They went back to the studio and Lillie made the children a Milo. She had an extra-strong instant coffee before returning to the fray.

As she walked back into the hall, she could see how prominent their set-up was. Robby Rob had crafted a long slender shape. He was now putting the finishing touches to the top. With his fingers theatrically sticking out he was carefully using his thumb and pointer to model the very top of …

"My God, he is making a penis!" Lillie whispered, looking around to see if anyone had noticed. Back on the stage she confronted Robby.

"What are you thinking? What are you doing?"

"Oh, just you wait until I have finished it!" he answered.

"Don't you dare put you-know-what with it!" she hissed

"No, no! It is not what you think. God, you women, is that all you think about? Ha! Just wait until it is finished!"

Lillie was not convinced. She did not trust him, and he smelled of drink!

Robby created two more, long, slender pots, each one with a different top. The three were then pushed together. He found some long grass to top off the beauty of his vases. All went well. Their display and the demonstrations got a mention in the Castlemaine Mail. There was also a picture of Lillie surrounded by children. The local population started to accept them as nice weirdoes. Now and then a local would come into the shop to buy a pot or to have a chat.

Their little shop filled up with work from local crafts people. Some paintings, leatherwork and jewellery mingled with the pottery. Lillie loved being surrounded by other artists' work. She could enjoy the beautifully crafted items, and sometimes even dream of owning one of them. She fell in love with a silver ring in the shape of a fish with a small ruby as an eye. Would they ever be able to afford something like that?

With all the new works in the shop Lillie had to learn to be a bookkeeper. Oh, only she had been more attentive in bookkeeping class at the photographic college. Numbers were a complete enigma to her. But she had to learn, gain knowledge of numbers and work out how to keep them all in order. She bought a notebook, nominated one side for the incoming money and the other for expenses. It worked.

One day she was asked if they took lay-by. She had no idea what lay-by meant. Excusing herself from the customer she went to the next-door' shop for advice. The man wanted to buy a leather handbag for his partner. Her birthday was in four weeks and he wandered if a small deposit would do to secure the bag? Lillie got her account book and entered the customer's name and the amount paid. Proudly she handed a receipt to Mr. N. Shard. From then on, every morning Neil Shard dropped in with his scruffy, black dog, Gorky, a meat pie and a small bottle of brandy. He seemed to know Roby Robb. Settling down at the table in the workshop he would make himself a cup of coffee with a good shot of brandy in it, then feed the pie to the dog. Soon Robby's coffee would also be flavoured with brandy and that just before class! Every morning irritated Lillie had to throw them out of the workshop. Neil never brought any money! Four weeks later his partner came to pay for her birthday present.

Day after day Neil kept on dropping in with his dog, brandy, and pie. Smiling at Lillie, who was far too busy to notice, he lifted his brandy laced coffee cup and then engaged Robby Rob in deep conversation.

Robby Rob, on the other hand, went from being a charming, helpful guy to a charming, lazy drunk. By midday he was quite bubbly, by the afternoon sentimental, then by the evening he had to be pulled out of one of the pubs, where he ended up drinking the slops. The drinking became more important in his life than the work in the pottery.

"Time for a divorce," Callan told him one day.

Robby Rob hopped on his pushbike and disappeared. They never saw him again.

Lillie missed his company and his maddening irresponsible attitude to life. He had somewhat brought a slightly moronic atmosphere into their very sensible and ordered life. He had been a good mate. She often wondered what happened to him.

BOX SEVEN

'Under Milkwood Downunder', Callan had called it. There were no cobbled streets or a fishing-boat bobbing sea. Yes, the nights were bible-black, the houses looked as blind as moles, but there was no Captain Cat or Mr. Owen. There was, though, Mr. Hayes in his shoe shop, and Ivor Sampson the draper. The young postman, Cook, who used to sneak onto their property and then report to the townsfolk what the hippies on the corner were doing. There was Jimmy Bow and Bill Benstead, the grocers, working at Brooks store just up the road from them. Yes, Maldon once was an Australian 'Under Milkwood'.

Lillie thumbs through the big bulging box of photos. She finds an old picture of their Maldon house taken in the late 1800s. She loved that house. They lived in it for twenty-five years. What a busy life they created there. They filled the building with noise and laughter. With them the old sombre building became alive again. Lillie smiles thinking about that time.

A HOUSE OF THEIR OWN

Following the agent's car through the avenue of elm trees, they turned right into Maldon's Main Street. It was like the street of a ghost town with most of the shops closed. Many of them had their windows hung with brown paper or old curtains. Some of the places looked deserted and in great need of repair. Callan put the car into low gear to be able to take in the feel of the 'village', as he called it.

On the very top of Main Street was a large intersection. On the corner a big white house with a shop attached. It also looked unoccupied. The wide road gave it the feeling of not belonging to the place. It looked as if it did not want to be part of the town.

The agent turned left at the junction. She then turned the car around and parked outside the insignificant, small, grey door of the white house. Callan did not believe his eyes. This was the house he had fallen in love with on that cold, rainy Queen's Birthday long weekend two years ago.

There was no bell or doorknocker to announce that they had arrived. The agent just went in and called out.

"Yoohoo! Anyone home?"

The most beautiful brick paving greeted them. They had walked into a kind of breezeway. The house and its front door were on their right; on the left a high brick wall with steps leading up to a building, the old bakery. At the end of the house, framed by the veranda, the paving widened, and on a small rise they could see a two-storeyed old brick stable.

"Please come in."

A tall lady had opened the door to the house. She stood in the dark corridor. With the small amount of light falling on her, Lillie saw a rather stern, sharp-featured face. She was quite thin. Maybe in her sixties? It seemed to Lillie that this lady would not tolerate nonsense. She did not introduce herself.

The front door was rather narrow, and they slowly filed into the long corridor and from there into the large kitchen on the left. There was a small gas stove and a sink with a bench covered in fruit-decorated plastic, a table and some chairs. The walls, the doors, the window frames, the ceiling and the mantlepiece were all painted in the same off-white colour. On the wall, by the stove, one could see the result of many years of cooking. One quite large window faced out to the brick entrance, the other to the garden. They were hung with layers of curtains. The floor was a patchwork of linoleum-scraps. There was a light bulb hanging from the high ceiling. The room felt unused.

Opposite the kitchen door was one of the four bedrooms. All the windows were facing the street. The house sat right at the edge of the footpath. One probably could sit in bed and shake hands with a passer-by! The windows were of a different design to the kitchen. The owner pointed out to them that this was the oldest part of the building, probably from the 1860s.

In one of the rooms the thick render had peeled off. Someone had crudely repaired the wall by slapping cement over the faulty part. The bare floors showed well-worn, but beautiful old floorboards. The ceilings were still in their original dark-stained wooden boards. Lillie enquired why the last room was so much bigger. And she wanted to know why there was a little window leading into the corner-shop.

"I think this was the office. Through the window the shopkeeper could watch the customers," the tall lady explained.

The room next to the kitchen was the large living-room. It looked newly-painted. The fluorescent light flickered on and revealed pink walls, a large dark green rug, a big couch, armchairs, a TV, coffee table, a glass cabinet with trinkets and glasses. There was also a large fireplace, the mantlepiece missing; the brick arch partially destroyed to make room for a heater. On either side of the fireplace there were windows, again hung with all kinds of curtains. It felt as if the inhabitants were afraid of letting the view of the garden in.

In one of the armchairs Lillie could see the head and shoulders of a man. As the light came on, he stood up to greet them. He was a little taller than his wife, with a round body. His brown face and his strong physique made it hard to guess his age. He was dressed in working clothes.

"Jack Wolstcroft." With a big smile he introduced himself. "Do you like our house? Did Margaret show you all the rooms? Have you been in the shops, looked at the garden and the outhouses? You must."

He slowly led them via the corridor to the large shop, from there into a smaller one and out into the garden. He invited them to go and look at the property. To take their own time. To have a good stickybeak.

At the back of the house was a large veranda, also brick-paved;

beyond that, between the house and the stable, untidy grass and two apricot trees. On the left of the brick path, which led to the stable, a low-brick wall. On the left up a few big stone steps an outside toilet. A well-used track went through the whole property. It entered from the street by the stable gates to exit at the back of the old bakery into the street where they had parked their car.

Callan and Lillie went their own ways to inspect the large property. Lillie wanted to have a look at the old bakery building. It was an excellent space for a studio. She could see where one could have a vegetable garden. The stable was ideal for their goat, Vickie. Attached to the stable were a number of outbuildings. All brick! Jammed between the stable and the large shed was a small, longish room with no windows. Immediately Lillie thought of a darkroom. She had missed her photographic work. This was the perfect place! The last shed had a little opening leading out. This would make a great place for the chickens. In her mind she had already moved in, working out where everything would go. She never thought of asking the agent about important things ... like how big was the place, and how much?

Lillie's parents never owned a house. She grew up in a large, old, rented apartment in Vienna; where she was born and lived until leaving home at the age of 19. Just the thought of owning a property like this made her feel extremely excited. She wanted to have it, live here; turn this mess into a beautiful garden. Involve her children in the beginning of this new chapter in her life!

Callan went to inspect the stable. It was in its original condition with two stalls for horses. No steps led up into the loft. It was a great solid building and surely useful for something in the future. He looked at all the buildings, checking their condition. Wandering about the garden he came across some old car bodies. Feeling that it was already his property he thought, 'They must go! Strange how Australians always have to have a rubbish corner!'

Lillie had caught up with him.

"I love it. This austere white facade revealing all that! What do you think?" she said.

But Lillie knew his answer; she could read it in his eyes. They both knew that they would never be able to afford such a big place. They had not thought of asking for the price of the property before looking at it!

With his arm around her shoulder Callan walked Lillie back into the house, where they met up with the owners and the agent. All looked at them in great anticipation.

"Well," said Jack Wolstcroft, "What do you think? Now to business. We are asking $15,000."

Callan and Lillie looked at each other. Lillie could feel her whole body getting weak. It felt as if something extremely beautiful had been held in front of her. It was out of reach. It was not for her to have.

"Sorry, but we just haven't that sort of money," Callan replied.

"How much can you afford?" Mrs. Wolstcroft asked.

"Well ..." Callan started, embarrassed, "We have $9.000. But probably can get a loan, taking it to $12,000."

"Done!" said Mrs. Wolstcroft. Looking hard at them with her sharp eyes she asked. "Aren't you potters?"

They all turned towards her. Her husband's face was a big question mark. The agent stepped back. She felt that there was very little for her to add to the negotiation. Margaret Wolstcroft continued, looking at her husband,

"You see, love, they have $9.000. We could just lend them the rest until they get it from the bank. They look like honest people and then they might just be some competition to that Mr. Wilson!"

Jack walked to the cabinet, took out some glasses and a bottle of sherry. He filled the small, elegant glasses and handed them around.

Raising his glass, he said, "Cheers! May the house be good for you. I am looking forward getting to my recently purchased farm. Cheers!"

Lillie sipped her sherry. She was not very fond of the sweet variety. Actually, she did not like sherry at all; champagne would have been a good celebratory drink. Then she looked at Mrs. Wolstcroft.

"Sorry, Mrs. Wolstcroft, but what did you mean when you asked us if we were potters? And who is Mr. Wilson?"

"Mr. Burnell is a big unpleasant man with no regards to anyone but himself!" She looked at Lillie and continued, "Mr. Burnell's mother owns the two shops down from the garage. The building with the Bushel sign she uses as a milk bar, the other one is empty. Well, she let us have the empty shop for our community op shop. Now, Mr. Burnell has just finished his pottery degree in Bendigo and will be taking over the shop. We have still got one month in which to sell what we have. It is all for a good cause and the money goes back into the community! Now, this brute of a man has already moved his pottery wheel in. He makes fun of us ladies by putting on the frocks for sale and, to top it off, hats and scarves! He is too big for most of the clothes, and many have been ripped. Then he sits in the window, all dressed up, making his pots. Showing off! Keeping the customers away!"

Her reserved, stiff shell had fallen off. Maybe it was the sherry? Mrs. Wolstcroft became extremely excited. Jack put his arm around her. He tried to calm his wife.

"I am sure the Pennington's will become stiff competition for Mr. Burnell."

"We will do our utmost," Callan replied." Competition is always a good thing."

The agent left them standing outside the grey door of the house, their new home to be. For a long time they stood and just looked down the street. It was mid-winter. The branches of the elm trees drew black lines into the brilliant blue sky. The town was surrounded by soft, green hills covered in eucalypts trees. There was not a soul to be seen; not a car drove through the streets. To them it felt like being in a time-warp.

Callan broke the stillness. "Let's go for a wander."

Going up the road they came to a General Store, after that nothing much, just a small church hall and houses.

Going down the street they ended up by the Post Office. Two cars were parked outside the building. The cars were side-by-side, the two drivers in deep conversation. Out of the old Post Office building, pushing hard on one of the double doors, an old man appeared, carrying a small parcel.

"I wonder when they will do something to them doors," he mumbled as he joined the men in the cars. "Great weather we're having. A bit dry maybe, and cold, but what can you expect. It's winter." They carried on talking about the weather, ignoring the two strangers.

Callan and Lillie turned left past the shire offices and a small park with two magnificent oak trees, still in full leaf. The ground was littered with acorns. Just across the road Callan recognised the Kangaroo Hotel. During their first visit to Maldon he'd bought some bottles of wine there. Callan smiled as he thought of the barman's reaction. How he stuck his face over the bar and told Callan, "Blokes drink beer"!

"Let's have a beer!" Callan suggested, "Let's see if the barman recognises me."

Lillie did not like beer. 'I wonder if he will let me have a glass of wine?' she thought.

The bar was empty. But then it was a bit early for a drink. Callan looked at the barman.

"One beer and a glass of dry white, please."

"Coming up," was the answer and, as the drinks were poured, "Aren't you the one who bought all that red wine, some two years ago?"

He looked at the two and introduced himself.

"Matt Cox is the name. What brings you back?"

Proudly they said, "We have just bought a house in Maldon. This is a celebratory drink! Cheers. Have one yourself."

"Too early for me! What did you buy and why would you want to come and live in this godforsaken, forgotten town? It's full of pensioners, old folk. They like the climate here, much warmer than Castlemaine and cheaper than Bendigo. Just look at their gardens, beautiful. That's all they do. Gardening, a bit of bowls, not much more. On the other hand, new blood, a young family, would do the town the world of good. Anyway, good luck. By the way, what did you buy?"

After they proudly told him he just looked at them and shook his head.

"Well, good luck. That place hasn't been good for anyone. Enjoy your drink."

And with those words he went back to studying his paper.

They finished their drinks and carried on down the street until they came to a big Y-intersection.

"Well, at least there's a garage and a petrol station." Callan felt progress.

Wandering up Main Street, through the shopping centre, towards 'their' house, they noticed a milk bar with a small shop attached, where one could buy some groceries. Across the road a fish-and-chip place and a newsagency. There was a barber with a 'book exchange' table and then, not to be missed, the two-storey Maldon Hotel. There was also a butcher. The rest of the shops seemed empty. And then they were back at the big white house.

When living in Maldon they discovered many more shops. Ivor Sampson with his draper's shop; Mr. Hayes soled shoes; the chemist, Harvey Loftus, who delivered prescriptions to 'the oldies' with his Vespa Scooter. Choocky Pollard ran the newsagency; Arch Martin and his wife, Marj, lived in a rickety two-storeyed shop, with the residence upstairs, and sold 'old wares' in the shop below. Maldon had three garages, three pubs and three churches. There was a large Primary School and a kindergarten. Brooks' Store, just up the road from their house, sold everything from chicken food to coffee. They certainly could get anything they needed without the use of a car.

The bank manager looked at them long and hard.

"I could not possibly give you a loan for a house that is over 100 years old! No matter how solid, no matter how big, no matter that it is made of brick! Sorry, but No!"

They had got all dressed up! Walked into the bank manager's office full of confidence. Now they felt totally deflated! What to do?

"I can recommend a reliable solicitor who will be able to help you with a loan," he added.

He handed them a name and address. "Give him a ring and make an appointment. Or if you like I can ring him?"

He rang and wrote the time and date next to the address.

L. Langslow sat behind his very large, antique desk and was in the process of cutting up envelopes. There was a small pile of them already on his desk with a large gemstone holding them in place. He was an elderly man. His wife had attended their classes for a few months.

"Please sit down. My wife did enjoy your classes. She now has a new interest. Not too sure what it is. It could be flower arrangements. Can't keep up with her hobbies. Well, what can I do for you?"

He picked up one of the cut-up envelopes and started writing.

"They make excellent scrap-papers," he explained.

After they had told him their plans, made him aware about the fact they owned land, had a registered business and anything else that could interest him, they asked him for a loan. He just smiled and told them his plan.

"Yes, I can get you the money. My suggestion would be that you give me two repayments a year. I feel, that is the best way. You nominate the best times."

Having absolutely no idea about loans and repayments, they agreed. All Callan and Lillie wanted was to get the money to buy the house!

"I will draw up a contract for you to sign. Let's say in ten days?"

He shook their hands and bid them goodbye.

"Well, that was easy!"

At the end of July they took possession of the white house on top of Main Street in Maldon.

There were already cars with trailers parked outside the big white house on the top of Main Street, waiting for Lillie and Callan to tell them what to do, where to leave the few possessions. The grey door was not locked. There was no one about. Some of the helpers walked into the now completely empty, very sad looking house. One of them ventured into the kitchen.

"What a dump! How much did you say you paid for this heap of bricks?"

Standing in the doorway of the kitchen, Callan and Lillie looked at the patchwork of linoleum. Should they leave it or remove it?

"What a great picture that floor is," someone said.

"We remove it!" was Callan's reply.

With whatever tools they could muster, thousands of tacks were removed. Under the linoleum patchwork they found a thick layer of old newspapers. Someone started reading.

"Listen, this paper is from 1952! I wasn't even born!"

"Take it home and read it! We haven't got all day!"

The noise of pulling up papers continued. Carefully the old news was placed in a pile to be read later. Working her way towards the sink, Lillie found that the papers were feeling damp and, further on, quite wet. She discovered that the overflow of the small, electric-hot water service was leaking onto the floor.

'This has to be fixed ASAP,' she thought.

Someone discovered a hole, covered with a bit of tin, under a pile of newspapers. No one said anything. They just worked away quietly.

"This is a beautiful old floor. These boards are very old. Look at the width of them. When fixed, sanded and polished this will be a great floor." Someone observed.

The work was done. The linoleum bits lay in a pile outside on the brick paving, the newspapers carefully bundled up. Now the furniture could be brought in; a dresser, a number of fruit boxes, Dante's Trunk, the fridge and one chair; the double bed, the cot and a few mattresses. The children were running up and down the long corridor trying to pick a room.

"I want the one with the little window!"

"No that's mine!"

"Who would like a pie?" Lillie shouted over the noise

Lillie had been down to the bakery and bought everyone a pie. The quietness was only broken by strange sucking sounds and complaints about having burned their mouths.

"Pies are supposed to be hot, mate!"

There was no gas or power on. They could not make tea. Callan went down the pub for a slab of beer. The job was done.

Lillie looked at the old wood stove.

"If we all go and look for sticks in the garden, I can light a fire and cook some dinner."

"Do we have some food to cook?" Callan replied. "There are no shops open at this hour in this little village!"

They went to "Joe's Fish n' Chips Emporium". This was their first and last visit to that establishment. Never had they tasted such rancid, greasy food. Even the cigarette papers Callan bought there tasted of rancid fat.

As beautiful as the drive from Maldon to Castlemaine was, this morning Lillie did not enjoy it. She would have much rather stayed at home. Stuart had to be taken to school in Castlemaine, Jane to kindergarten, Liam to Margaret Harrison to be babysat. Pottery orders needed to be filled. She still had a few months doing her work in Castlemaine. Sitting at the pottery wheel this Monday morning, confronting a large pile of clay to be turned into mugs, she realised that every pot would mean money for the payment of the house. Just to pass the time more quickly Lillie tried to work out how many mugs she would have to make to repay their debt. With a shudder she gave up when she reached a thousand. Time passed quickly. Soon the shelves in the studio filled up with mugs. Tomorrow she would put all the handles on. But now it was time to pick up the children.

"Home we go," she said to Stuart when she picked him up from school.

He found it hard having to leave his friends behind. "You will be back tomorrow and the day after and the day after! Is it not exciting to go home to our very own house, to your very own room?"

Arriving at her house she was greeted with total chaos. Callan had not managed to get the power, or the gas put on. He and Allan had worked all day collecting rocks for an extension to be built onto the old bakehouse which was not big enough to house the kiln.

"What are we doing for dinner? Fish-and-chips again?"

"I am not having any more of those disgusting, greasy chips. And I will never ever have fish again!" Lillie had a mutiny on her hands.

"OK. Go and find some wood. There must be some about this place, nothing longer than your foot. I will cook on the wood stove. Let's hope it works!"

The stove worked like a charm. Soon the family sat around Dante's Trunk enjoying their first home cooked meal in their new house.

The following day Callan and Allan continued building the stone wall which was to be attached to the old historic bakery. They had never constructed a stone wall before. Total concentration was needed, the right stones found.

"Excuse me, but do you have a building permit for the work you are doing?"

Startled Callan looked over the low wall.

"No, why?"

"Can I please see the owner of this property?"

Callan glanced at the official-looking man and introduced himself. He did not have time for any interruption. The kiln was soon going to be moved from Castlemaine. This shed needed to be finished!

"A building permit for a shed?"

"Yes, you need a building permit for a building. I feel that is what you are doing!"

"How long will that take? I need to get this finished so I can get my kiln built and get on with our work!" Callan made a frustrated gesture. Allan just kept on working.

With great interest the shire engineer started to ask Callan a host of questions. He walked around the small wall into the emerging room to find out how the wall was built. The inspector smiled when he saw the uneven state of the building effort.

"Well, I can see you have never built a stone wall before! Still, it looks quite solid. Listen, what we will do … you get that permit lodged but keep on working. When I need to come past your place, I'll look the other way. When you eventually get the permit, I will come and inspect your very interesting stone walls."

"You know," the man said in parting "Your building could be as old as the bake house it is attached to. Looks very authentic. Yes, I like it."

The kiln-room was built and approved by the authorities. The engineer actually quite liked the stonework and the little second-hand window, which did not sit quite straight in the wall. He signed the official papers and wished the Pennington's the best of luck in their new venture.

"We are almost in business." Callan waved the form as he entered the kitchen. "All we need now is the delivery of the gas tank."

With the help of their friends the enormous task of moving the pottery started. The kiln had to be pulled down, brick by brick. They created a chain of people from the kiln to the cars. As the bricks arrived in Maldon it was Lillie's task to clean the dry, hardened clay slurry from each of them. Then they had to be stacked in neat piles close to the new kiln room, which was still roofless. A large tarpaulin was strung over the roof frame. There was no money to buy any roofing iron.

The bakery now looked like a pottery studio. The wheels had been moved and Lillie was busily working, stocking up for Christmas. All they needed was the kiln and gas.

The permit to get a gas tank had still not arrived. It seemed that there was a problem between the gas company and the National Trust.

"Why the National Trust?" Callan asked the building inspector. "What do they have to do with approving gas tanks?"

He was told that the Shire of Maldon gave the National Trust the power to decide on building matters in the classified part of Maldon and their house was in the A-classification.

"How does that affect us and our gas tank?" Callan's voice sounded very worried.

There was a problem with the colour of the tank. White was not permitted in the A-classified part of Maldon. It had to be off-white. The gas company insisted that all tanks have to be white — not off-white — to reflect the sun. The National Trust suggested they bury the tank. Or have it hidden behind a building? No, the tank had to be seen from the gas tanker when refilling, said the gas company. The argument went back and forth, and no result was found. The engineer invited the National Trust to come and see the problem. A visit to Maldon was long overdue.

Three black-suited men came in a chauffeur-driven car. Walking about the chosen area for the tank, they busied themselves with tape measures, writing things down, waving their arms about and also taking some photographs. They declined a cup of coffee and climbed back into their car. And drove off.

Half the street stood outside the Scotch Pie House wondering what the result of the visit would be. If the young new family could not start their pottery venture, would they have to leave Maldon? The town just could not afford to lose a young family. They would have to do what country folk were very good at: Helping. Brook's store offered them credit, so did the garage and the chemist. During the weeks of waiting and watching their bank balance dwindle this took most of the stress away, still Lillie felt a slight panic rise when she thought of the deadline of the Christmas orders.

Then the big day arrived. Watching the one-ton gas tank hanging and swinging from the thick chain as it was slowly manoeuvred into their property sent a tingling excitement through Lillie. She admired the skill of the crane operator as he gently placed the tank on the prepared concrete slabs. The tank was released from its chain, which now happily danced about, hanging from the big hook on the crane. Norm, the gasfitter, was ready to connect the copper pipes to the kiln filled with pots waiting to be fired.

The kiln room by now had a roof. Lillie's mother had given them a present of $45, which was immediately spent on secondhand tin for the 'lid', as Callan called it. The following day Callan fired the kiln. They were in business again.

Still Lillie's thoughts were heavy and troubled. They should have been finished two months ago. Was she too late? Christmas was the time where they had most of their sales. The packing-up of their life in Castlemaine, the moving of their studio, the decision to stop teaching, the looming of their first payment of the house. A slight panic entered Lillie. Then there was the family and the life that came with it. Stuart and Jane were happy at the Maldon Primary school,

Liam spent a few hours at the kindergarten.

'All will be well ... somehow,' she thought as she looked at the pile of prepared clay next to her. It was after eight in the evening. The children were bedded down. That was the time when their work started. Having decided to work at night gave them the opportunity to be with their children after school. She looked at Callan who smiled at her and jokingly remarked,

"It's either that pile of clay to be transformed into mugs or getting a job at the Castlemaine Bacon Factory!"

Callan, who was firing the kiln, was working on some new glazes. In front of him lay large slivers of yellow-box bark, beautiful grey-white with some green and brown stripes. He was setting out to copy the colours of the bark. Lillie could hear him mumble to himself. He sounded like a chef creating a new dish.

"To get the grey I'll try 3-5% of Yellow Oxide and about 3% of Titanium mixed in the clear glaze. That should give me a grey. Yes, I'll give it a go. Maybe another test with ..."

He employed Lillie's grandmother's old cast-iron scales, the weights in a beautiful wooden box. The scales were badly balanced, and he used bits of dry clay to even out the brass dishes, making sure the needle was in the middle.

By ten in the evening the pile of clay had been turned into mugs. Callan felt the rhythm of his wife as she threw one ball of clay on the wheel to turn it into a mug, then the wheel stopped to remove the finished pot and a slap as the next ball hit the pottery wheel; slap, stop, slap. It took her under a minute to make a mug.

Soon the shelves were filled with boards full of pots, glistening and wet. She stood up and had a good stretch.

"Smoko!" she said as she walked out of the studio to get them a cup of tea.

They sat on the steps to the old bakehouse, now their studio. The December night was balmy. Through the open studio door, a strip of light fell on the unkempt garden. As if in a meditative state Callan slowly took the Drum tobacco out of his pocket and rolled them each a cigarette. Both were looking at the black nothing of the night.

"What's next?" Callan broke the silence.

"Probably bowls. How long until the kiln goes off?"

"She'll be another two hours. I'll help you prepare the clay."

By three in the morning they knocked off.

"Better cover up the pots with some plastic. Otherwise, the heat of the kiln will dry them too fast. Tomorrow we'll put the handles on and finish the bowls."

Callan turned the lights off and they walked back inside the house where they enjoyed a slice of bread and a glass of, "Chateau Vin Vale".

Bed felt good. Maldon was fast asleep.

In the morning the children would stand at the end of their bed. It was eight in the morning. Jane was pulling on the blanket. They had got themselves up and made their own breakfast.

"Mum! Liam put a whole lot of Milo under the cornflakes."

Lillie looked at her three children through tired eyes. She had to smile. She was proud to see how they managed at such a young age.

"Liam's jumper is inside out and Jane it is too cold to wear your new thin dress you got from Gran. And somehow the boots do not go too well with your outfit. Stuart, you'll do. See you at lunchtime."

With that she turned to the wall, cuddled under her blanket, and managed to get a little more sleep. The children loved their mornings without parents. They all took far too much Milo and far too little of anything else. Liam did not like milk. He was happy not to have his mother pester him to put some on his breakfast.

Reluctantly Jane would take little brother Liam up the road to kindergarten. It was one of her jobs to do so. Otherwise, no pocket money!

Stuart met his friends on the way to school. Children came from all directions. Like a small swarm of bees, they walked off to school, kicking stones or abandoned cans, their raucous noises dampening as they entered the school grounds.

The small tribe of children mingled outside the school building, waiting for the bell to call them to attention. The loudspeaker would blare out its scratchy, tired marching music making the small group stride around the front of the school. It sounded as if it was played in a tin can. Someone inside the building removed the needle from the record. The music suddenly stopped. The little parcel of children marched up the steps to be swallowed up by the dark doorway of the old school.

There were only two teachers, the headmaster being one of them. Even though the townsfolk felt that the Pennington's were a very strange lot, the arrival of their children was extremely welcome. They might now get a third teacher. Also, with the enrolment of Liam in the kindergarten there was now a future for this fledgling kindergarten with its handful of children. Most of the helpers in this establishment were volunteers and parents.

It was Lillie's turn to do the 'fruit duty' at the kindergarten. Standing in the tiny kitchen, listening to the chatter of a group of little girls, she started peeling the oranges.

"No, no, no! We do not peel the oranges. We peel the apples and cut the oranges into segments like that."

Mrs. Long, the teacher, showed her how it was done. She put some of the cut orange segments on a little plate with the peeled apple quarters.

"Like that, Mrs. Pennington!"

Lillie proceeded to peel the apples. It made her think of her mother and she could hear her say," All the sunshine is in the peel. Eat your peel!" Lillie looked at the long curl of the apple peel lying on the bench. She picked it up at one end and started to slowly chew it, pulling the curl into her mouth. Soon the little plates were filled with apples and oranges. Mrs. Long looked at her with a satisfied smile. Then, "What did you do with the apple peel?!"

"I ate it. It is good for you. It is full of sunshine."

Mrs. Long, a rather large lady suddenly seemed to be larger.

"I wanted the peel for my chooks!"

She looked at Lillie and just shook her head.

Lillie was never asked to do the fruit again. She was put into the category of a strange lady from a faraway country where they eat apple peel.

To stretch the household money, Lillie tried her luck at bread making. Her attempts were not appreciated by the family. Stuart suggested that the loaves would make great doorstops, Jane hated it and wanted a pie, just like her friend, Rhonda, who got money from her mother every day to buy lunch. It was hard to explain to a six-year-old that money was scarce in this household.

Callan had gone down to the Post Office with a pocketful of coins to phone their clients. He came home with the devastating news that their work was not needed. They were too late. The shops had been stocked well for Christmas.

This lunchtime Lillie sliced her hard, homemade bread very thinly. There was some cheese, butter and jam. Putting the offerings on a plate in the middle of Dante's Trunk she looked at her children, walked out into the garden and lit a cigarette. Had she failed her children? Did they do the wrong thing by dragging them away from a secure living situation in Melbourne? Walking up and down, taking deep drags, she kept on blaming herself.

Callan had stayed with the children, concerned he watched her through the window. He never showed his frustrations, but he was also worried. They would have to load up the car with their wares and go selling. Could they afford the petrol? The children ate their lunch in total silence and without complaining. They could feel the heavy atmosphere. They knew something was wrong.

Liam was in bed having his afternoon sleep, Stuart and Jane back at school. Callan went out to join Lillie in the garden. Nervously she started talking about having to start living off the garden produce and eggs and maybe kill a chicken now and then. The big IF of their future hung heavily over Lillie. Trying to calm her he put his arm around her.

"Why don't we pack up the car and try to sell what we have? Allan can look after the children. If we leave early, we can be back by dinnertime. Maybe with no pottery and a fat check."

The station wagon was packed, one box with samples in easy reach. Callan had created new glazes. They were trying to get away from the earthy stoneware look of the day. The reds and blues and greens surely should catch some shopkeeper's eye. Then there were the blue and white decorated mugs. Lillie took great care in choosing the best of their pottery.

Even though it was still dark when they left, one could feel that the day was going to be a hot one. Thanks to the credit offered by the local garage the tank of the Toyota was full. Callan was very grateful that the Calder Highway was almost empty; being the middle of the week helped. By Kyneton the radio faded, and Lillie put a tape on. Full of hope to be coming home with some money both were singing to the familiar music.

As they drove through Woodend and into the Black Forest the sun was well up. Usually, they would stop in Gisborne for a coffee. Not today! Lillie had packed lunch. There was just no money to be spent on a little luxury like coffee.

The traffic started to thicken. Some country-seeking 'Melburnians' had moved out of the City into the countryside to enjoy the quietness of a few acres of nature. They commuted to work. The drive became slower and slower, the highway filled up with cars. As they drove into Sunbury, once a small country town nestled amongst green hills. Now the landscape had been turned into a sprawling suburb. Lillie started to hum: "Little boxes on the hillside, little boxes made of ticky-tacky, little boxes, little boxes, little boxes all the same …".

"Look at all those terrible houses, just like mushrooms popping up everywhere. I don't think they were here last time we drove through Sunbury."

Lillie looked in horror at the development. The destruction of good land, green and lush. Melbourne was growing. The roads had not been improved to accommodate the increasing traffic. Then Melbourne swallowed them up. Callan's mood changed.

"Christ, I hate Melbourne."

They were driving from client to client, but no one was interested in buying. No one needed their wares.

"Sorry, we are well-stocked. Lovely colours. Maybe next year?" they heard all day.

Just as they were turning the car towards home, they saw a small craft shop in Lygon Street. This was going to be their last try. Irritated Callan was looking for parking.

"Just double-park and let me out!" Lillie yelled.

She grabbed the box full of samples and walked into, 'Rosie's'.

"No thank you, I am stocked up to the hilt!" An elderly lady stood behind the counter.

Lillie managed to get her to at least look at what they were producing, maybe for some other time? The lady pursed her lips and studied their offerings.

"Is all your stuff like that?"

Lillie felt her heart drop.

"Yes, more or less."

"How much have you got?"

"A car full!"

"I'll take the lot!"

Lillie almost fainted. She was totally exhausted from smiling and being polite and charming to all the shopkeepers she had met during the day. As they unpacked Rosie examined every pot, muttering about the beauty of the colours.

"Thank you for coming. Look at my shelves. All brown pottery! Your work will brighten up this dreary place."

Rosie became a very reliable client, always helping them out of financial corners. Lygon Street was the street where Callan and Lillie used to meet for lunch before they were married. Callan coming from Allan Studios in Smith Street, and Lillie from the University just up the road. Lygon Street was the street where Callan slowly divorced himself from 'The Old Country' and started to embrace a future in Australia, a future with Lillie. It seemed such a long time ago. So much had happened since their innocent courtship.

They could now settle their debts, and Christmas, which was only a few weeks away, would be a happy one. All the way home, Lillie made plans for their first Christmas celebrations in their very own house. In her mind she spruced up a tree with the few decorations she had brought with her from Vienna. They could make more, maybe bake some gingerbread biscuits. Her happiness made her mind run wild.

A round advent calendar was hanging from the high ceiling. Callan had to put a ladder on Dante's Trunk to reach the ceiling so he could hang Lillie's invention. The ring was a polystyrene frame used to make wreaths. The ugly polystyrene was disguised with short pine branches. Twenty-four matchboxes were glued on the underside of the ring. In every matchbox was a small present: one for each December day. Liam, the youngest, had the first pick, the first little draw; the first little surprise on the first of December 1974.

Lillie glanced around the very sparsely furnished room. The boxes around Dante's Trunk, their dining table.

"I would like to eat our Christmas dinner off a proper table. What about if we give ourselves and the house a table-present?" Lillie looked at Callan.

He just smiled and added, "Then we need some chairs as well."

At Cassidy's secondhand store in Castlemaine, they found a round table. Once upon a time one could extend it, but the extension mechanism did not work. The top was quite scratched, then what do you expect for ten dollars? Jack felt it would look splendid covered with a colourful tablecloth. He added,

"Round tables are all the rage at the moment. No nasty mother-in-law corners," Jack tapped the side of his nose with his finger and smiled at Callan. "I can deliver if you like. No extra cost."

A round table was just the thing. They bought it.

"What are nasty mother-in-law corners?" Lillie asked on the way back to Maldon.

"They say, if you sit at a corner of a square table, you will get a nasty mother-in-law," Callan replied. "No problem here, your mother-in-law is in England."

Dante's Trunk was dragged into the living room and became a coffee table. The table arrived in the late afternoon.

"I found you four chairs. Can you afford another tenner? They are 1950'ish oak chairs from a restaurant."

Jack was holding one. It looked uncomfortable, with its very straight back.

"Well, chairs would be good. I am a bit sick of sitting on those old boxes. Why not! Let's go for broke!"

Callan took the chairs and put them with the table.

Jack got his money and a bag of Christmas biscuits.

"Happy Christmas to all of you. Have a good one."

Lillie and Callan worked out where to put the new acquisition. The kitchen looked more like a home without the boxes and the trunk. The boxes were stacked on top of each other and used as shelves. Later Lillie painted them in bright colours to cheer up the dreary kitchen.

"We have a new table?!" Jane was delighted and sat down on the chair. "Four chairs? Where is Liam going to sit, and Allan?"

"Liam on the highchair and Allan, well we do have the old 'Dutch' chair we bought before we were married," Lillie said.

Jane looked at her parents. "When am I going to get a proper bed? And my room fixed up and decorated?"

The parents looked at each other. "Soon. Let's just have Christmas first and then we can see."

Jane looked sternly at her parents. "Are we going to get a tree? With decorations? And lights? All the kids at school have trees already and the shops have been decorated for ages. When will we get a tree?"

"Yes, we will have a tree and decorations and lights, but not right now. It is a bit too early."

"Why? Why? Why do others have their tree?" Jane looked at her dad. He did not answer.

It was Christmas Eve. There was a tree with decorations and lights, the washing basket full of presents. The kitchen smelled of roast chicken. The children had laid the table with the silver cutlery Lillie had inherited from her grandmother. Christmas bonbons, crackers and sparklers decorated the table.

"Are we going to have a Christmas feast?" Jane danced around the table in her new dress. Picking a chair, she continued: "Why do we have so much cutlery next to our plate? Can I have one of those bonbons now? Do we have dinner or presents first? Oh, I am so excited!"

For starters Lillie had prepared a slice of ham with a few lettuce leaves and some tomato; then came Callan's gazpacho soup; then two roast chickens with potatoes and vegetables; and then a Pavlova, decorated by the children with flowers from the garden. It looked splendid.

With all the cheer and laughter, with the small explosions of the Christmas bonbons the old house became alive. The floor was littered with the discarded bonbon wrappers. Precariously all the extra paper crowns balanced on Callan's head. The children started to exchange the little items they got out of the bonbons, the adult read out the jokes.

After dinner Callan put on his Santa hat and handed out the presents. The children then played with their toys; the parents lifted their glasses.

"Cheers to our first Christmas in our own house!"

When the children were fast asleep, Callan snuck into their room with the sacks of presents. Presents only Father Christmas could afford.

The next day, Christmas Day, the family sat in the garden with last night's leftovers. Everyone was allowed to eat with fingers. "Picking time," Callan called it. On this day there was no talk of work or money or bills to be paid. Time out. Time off. A Holy Day. Christmas! Bliss!

Lillie and Callan were dozing under the apricot tree. It was warm and they felt lazy. Lillie was listening to her children playing on the swings Allan had built for them. Their laughter and squeals wafted towards her. On the happy noise of her children, she floated away. A call from Allan woke her.

"There is someone at the door for you."

A tall young couple came walking into the garden.

"Mike, my wife Jenny," the man said. "We would like to buy some of your pottery. I have opened a shop in Glen Iris and am looking for a potter. Maldon Pottery is closed for the Christmas holidays. Your door was open."

"Sorry, but we are having a day off. It is Christmas Day, is it not? Come back tomorrow and we will gladly show you our wares."

As Mike and Jenny walked away, Lillie looked at Callan.

"Today, is not a day for money-talk. Today is a holiday."

Watching the pair disappear through their front door, Lillie quietly continued:

"Bugger, I do hope he comes back! We need every penny!"

Mike and his wife did come back the next day. They looked like they had slept in their highly decorated VW van. Callan put the kettle on for a cup of coffee, Lillie brought a plate of cheese and bread out onto the veranda. Mike and Jenny had tried to find a cafe in Maldon, but everything seemed to be shut.

"Maldon seems to be all closed up. It gives you the feeling of a dead place." Jenny complained. "How can you live in a place like that?

Nothing seems to happen here!"

"That's why we love it here. Everything here feels real and honest. Also, the people here are incredible friendly and helpful." Callan offered her a cup of coffee. With a charming smile he added: "Milk and sugar?"

They found out that Mike was a leather worker with a degree in commerce. To live a life with less stress he had dropped out of the world of big business to set himself up with a craft shop. He was looking for pottery.

"Well, mate, you've come to the right place." Callan smiled and took them to see their wares.

Soon the floor of the storeroom was filled with their work. Mike carefully handled each item nodding in agreement of his choice. He looked at Callan.

"I like your shapes and I love your glazes. Who of you two is the potter?"

Callan pointed at Lillie.

"She does all the work on the wheel, the throwing. Together we put on the handles of the mugs. I do help finishing most of the pots. I make the glazes and fire the kiln. Lillie loads and unloads the kiln. We are partners in every aspect of life."

Michael smiled as he handed Lillie the cheque.

"I will see you next year. Yes, for sure I will!"

It was the last day of December. Callan sat on a chair staring at the wall which divided the kitchen from the bathroom, or the washhouse as the children called it.

"We badly need a door right here."

And with a thick black marker-pen Callan drew a large square on the wall. Then he put a big cross in the middle of the square. On the floor he had placed his stonemason's chisels and his short-handled, very heavy hammer. It was New Year's Eve.

"Yes, we badly need a door here!"

With resolute movements he picked up a chisel and the stumpy hammer and started attacking the large X on the wall. The old, thick plaster fell off like flaking skin.

"You are going to make all the plaster fall off!"

Lillie liked the thought of a door into the bathroom. But they needed a plan. She knew nothing about buildings and banging holes in walls. Callan put his tools down. Usually a very careful man, who would always plan before any action, he walked across to the table, poured himself another drink and admitted that a plan would be a good idea. He looked at his tools and decided on a large, flat, sharp chisel with which he gently marked the edges of the opening. Repeating this a number of times a groove appeared in the plaster.

Yes, Lillie liked the thought of a door just there. All winter the children had to run outside from the bathroom down the hallway and to the living room fire after their bath. And a proper bathroom would be great. The instant-gas hot water system blew up on the first attempt of running a bath, with dust and spiders flying out of the top of the old unit. It probably had not been used for a long time.

Outside the laundry/bathroom was a built-in fireplace with a big copper bowl for heating water. Allan explained to Lillie that in 'The Old Days' they heated up all the water in that contraption. They would boil their clothes in it as well.

'Not me', Lillie thought.

Cleaning out the firebox, Lillie managed to heat up some water then ladle it into the bathtub for the weekly bath. It reminded her of her childhood when, after the war, everything, including gas, was, as her father put it, "Frightfully expensive". They had baths with two children at a time. She remembered what a mess they made when fighting in the tub. She thought of her mother, who had six children. With that memory in mind her children would be washed one at a time, the last one always complaining about the temperature of the water.

After her three children had their bath, the water was bucketed into the old Pope washing machine for soaking the weekly clothes to be washed the next day.

It was New Years Eve. Callan was starting to make a door from the kitchen into the washhouse. The slow tapping of the mallet on the chisel had created a deep groove in the thick plaster. Lillie had put an old sheet on the floor to catch most of the debris. Callan was now standing on a chair. The top part was hard on his arm. He often stopped, shook his tired arm, wandered over to the table and had another sip of his beer.

Having finished scoring the outline of the opening, he gently started tapping on one corner. A whole sheet of plaster fell off, engulfing him in dust. Soon there was a perfect square cut out of the plaster revealing a solid, very well-built double brick wall.

The clock seemed to be speeding up. Callan wanted to have a hole in the wall by midnight. And he did. At midnight they managed to shake hands through a hole. They managed to clink their glass of Chateau Vin Vale Burgundy through the opening of the very solid double brick wall. This was the first change, the first remodelling of their new home.

"Happy New Year, my love! All the very best to us. I feel it will be a good one."

For a long time, she lay in bed that night next to her husband, who was fast asleep. The street, which was right outside the window, was still pumping the heat of the day towards the house and into the window. It was a hot, sultry night. Lying on top of her blanket she wished for a cool breeze. What sort of year would it be?

"Happy New Year!"

She could still hear Callan's cheerful voice. Why could she not feel the same positivity? The worries seem to be infinitely enlarged when lying in bed in the dark. The house payments were due next month. Maybe all will be better in the New Year. Sleep eventually came with the dawn.

"New Year does not feel any different!"

Liam woke them up.

"Hey, look at that mess in the kitchen. Are you starting to demolish our new house?"

"Wow, it's going to be a door, a door into the bathroom! No more running out in the cold after a bath! Are we now getting a proper bathroom?"

In the kitchen the children were hopping and dancing in the broken plaster and dust.

"Oh, please, stop that. You are walking this mess all over the place!"

In the cracks of the old wooden floor the dust had gathered. The children were grinding it into the old bare floorboards. Lillie was tired.

"Please go outside! Hop and dance outside. We'll have breakfast soon. Eggs and toast?"

They heard the flywire door slam against the door frame.

"Happy New Year!"

Their friend, Liz, walked into the kitchen.

"That looks interesting. Are you making a door there? Are you going to have a bathroom?" She laughed and hugged the children. "I have some news for you. You might like to sit down when I tell you."

Lillie made some coffee. They took their cups out and sat under the veranda.

"Have you heard? Mr. Langslow, the solicitor, dropped dead the other day, pushing his mower around his lawn in the middle of the day in that heat. Silly bugger he had a heart attack. Dead on the spot. Well, somehow a good way to go! Did you not borrow money from him?"

Almost dropping her mug Lillie looked at Callan. Slowly she got up, put her mug of coffee down and started a wild dance.

"Yes, yes, yes! Now I feel that this will be a happy New Year!" Throwing her arms up in the air she said, "Thank you! Thank you!"

Liz looked startled at Callan, who laughed.

"No, no she does not talk to the grey-haired, bearded man up there. It's just the sort of thing she does. Maybe inbuilt habit or it might just be in her DNA!"

All the exciting commotion brought the children and the dog onto the veranda. "What's the excitement?"

Barking, the dog waddled around Lillie. Liz looked at the size of the Beagle's belly.

"Yes, I am afraid there will be puppies." Callan did not sound very happy. "Not planned. A Labrador got at her."

"They will then be," Liz laughed. "A Beagle x Labrador? Well, there you are, a new breed of dog. I am sure the children will be thrilled."

"I will use that, Liz. I will advertise the 'Beagadors for sale. I can just see the advert in the local paper."

A few months later they received a letter from H.S.W. Lawson & Co., Solicitors asking them to come and see Mr. Bock. They were greeted by a highly irritated young solicitor.

"This is absolutely outrageous!"

Pointing at the contract in front of him on the desk.

"This is absolutely outrageous!" Spencer Bock repeated as he studied the documents Mr. Langslow had drawn up for them. "You would have never been the owner of your house the way he drafted this!"

He stood up from behind his desk, took his chair and sat next to Callan and Lillie.

"We had no idea, we totally trusted him."

"Well, he was a charming man. We will re-model your repayments to fit your income. If you could please give me some idea what your profit was last year? Maybe in the next few days?"

The embarrassment in both their face was very obvious. Profit what profit? They tried to explain.

"Look," he said. "It will take quite some time, maybe six months, before we get all Langslow's documents sorted out. I'll put yours on the bottom of the pile?"

A large lump of emotion had gathered in Lillie's throat. She could not talk. Her tongue was pressed hard against her palate, her teeth clenched to stop the tears of joy and relief.

"Thank you! That would be great."

Spencer stood up and shook their hand. "I will let you know. Don't worry, we'll look after you."

It was Monday and Lillie was going to do the washing. The children's clothes had been soaking in the old Pope washing machine all night. When it was time to put them through the wringer the device flew open, and the machine stopped. The wringer was broken. With great difficulty she heaved the washing into the bath and started to wring everything by hand. Callan popped his head into the washhouse asking if she needed anything from Castlemaine.

"Yes, I need a wringer for this dinosaurian washing machine. I saw a whole lot of them at the second-hand place. I could do with one of them. Please make sure it works!"

A hand with thumbs-up appeared through the new hole in the wall.

When Callan came back his face was beaming with excitement.

"I bought a piano. Jack will deliver it this afternoon! Oh, I will be able to play the piano again. And maybe the children would like to learn? I just had to have it! It only cost $100."

"And the wringer? Where is the wringer? And how much did you say the piano was? How are we going to pay for it?"

Without answering Callan ran out of the house and down to the Post Office. They did not have a phone. They could not afford such a luxury. He went to ring Jack at the second-hand shop from the public phone to bring a wringer.

The piano arrived. And the wringer. It was an upright grand, iron frame and extremely handsome. The question was where to put it. Callan wanted it across a corner so that the sound would be better. And away from the window. Lillie left them to it. She had washing to get on the line. The children needed their clothes. They did not have too many. As she was hanging up the washing, she could hear Callan tinkle the ivories.

The children did learn to play the piano. Mrs. Stacy the piano teacher, lived just down the street. She was one of those old-fashioned teachers with a ruler at the ready. Ready to smack little fingers which hit the wrong key. Stuart and Jane accepted her outdated approach, finishing all their grades with good marks. But Liam went on strike. He just loathed Mrs. Stacy, her ruler and her discipline.

As a child Callan had learnt to play the piano as well as the violin. He began to play again starting with simple tunes out of Carl Czerny's music book, the same music book the children learnt from. But mostly, he liked to make up his own tunes, which expressed his emotional state of the moment. Every evening, when everyone was in bed, he would settle down at the piano and let go of his feelings.

Lillie never played an instrument. Jokingly she would tell people that she only played the radio, and that she was very good at it. There was no time to learn the piano. Lillie instead learnt to master making jams out of their own fruit, as well as pickles and preserves from her garden produce. And after many failures, bread. She taught herself to spin wool. The process of creating a garment from the wool that came from a sheep's back, excited Lillie as much as making a functional vessel from a lump of clay. Her time was filled; filled to the brim with family, work, learning and discovering country life.

There was little time left where Lillie could disappear into her beloved world of photography. The camera very seldom was taken out of its leather case. Unprocessed films were waiting to be developed. The neglected darkroom equipment became covered in dust. There was no time to get lost in her pictures. Family and business were more important than her photography. The last image she captured, before selling her darkroom equipment, was of Stuart bursting with pride in his new high-school uniform. The faithful camera was stored away. The lid of Dante's Trunk stayed closed. It had been pushed into a corner. Dante's Trunk had been replaced by new furniture, by a new life.

BOX EIGHT

Lillie settles back, leaning against the trunk. Closing her eyes, she let her thoughts go to the years past. What wonderful times they had. Tears fill her eyes and turn the pile of pictures into an amalgam of out of focus greys, blacks and white. No, she will not put her life's memories out in the shed. She will keep them with her, close by her side. Somehow that way she feels that he will always be with her.

Very slowly she collects the photos which are strewn all over the floor and neatly puts them back into their allotted boxes. Each box representing a part of her life with Callan. And what a life it was. Many situations are not recorded. With a smile she thinks that not everything can be photographed. Many of the memories of her life with Callan were stored inside in her heart, deep in her psyche.

Box after box she slides back into the trunk. As Lillie puts the last box into the trunk, she can feel Callan by her side. It is the Agfa box filled with pictures from her childhood and the card Axel send her for her tenth birthday. The card that lured her to Australia from her home country on the other side of the world.

As Lillie closes the lid, she can almost feel Callan's hand on hers.

There is a place in the heart that
will never be filled
and even during the
best moments
and the greatest times
we will know it
more than ever
there is a place in the heart that
will never be filled,
and we will wait
and wait
in that space.

Charles Bukowski

www.ingramcontent.com/pod-product-compliance
Lightning Source LLC
Chambersburg PA
CBHW030257010526
44107CB00053B/1745